Punk Me

Poems and Other Bitchy Stuff

Patricia Hickerson

For Jon

Punk Me
Poems and other bitchy stuff by Patricia Hickerson

ISBN 978-1-105-09435-1

Published by Lulu.com

Interior layout by Craig Scott

Many of these poems have been previously published in *Rattlesnake Review*, *WTF*, *Echoes*, *Medusa's Kitchen*, *Convergence*, *Poetrynow*, *Primal Urge* and *The Ophidian*.

TABLE OF CONTENTS

1: CALL FOR LOVE

True Crime at Little York 1929   9
The Year of Being Thirteen   10
Spanish Influenza 1919   11
Strange 13
The Virgin Springs   14
Intemperance 15
Alcohol Dog   16
How She Rolls Into Her Game   17
August Her War 1944 18
Pursuit on W. 115th Street   19
Revlon Call for Love   20
Amsterdam Avenue 1949   21

2: HOW SHE ROLLS

Jessica at Cape May 2002   25
Riddle Me   26
Porn Star   27
Shape of Fred Haines (1936-2008)   28
Abyss 29
Explanation for the Man Still Waiting at the Corner   30
Tangomaster   31
Red Hot   32
High Times on Fillmore Street 1968   34
Dawn and Dirty   35
Rock Me   36
Softly Purring He Rapes Her Purse   37

3: STRANGE NIGHTS

Summer Night Swim   41
Just for a Minute   42
Height 43
Our Sheets Are Cool & Smooth   44
Spelling It Out 45
Funky Sun   46

Desperadoes   47
Romance   49
Frankie's Friend Eels   50
A Walk Through Vlad's Bucharesti   51
Murder on Park Avenue   52
We Return to That Street   53

4: FROM MY HOTEL WINDOW …

What I Saw from My Hotel Window on My 80th Birthday: 57
Comic Book Scenario 58
Triangle   60
Soldier 62
Take a Vacation   63
Like an Idiot…64
Penthouse Magazine in Afghanistan   65
Free Fall to Love   66
Memory of My Dancer   67
My Dog is Now My Lover   68
Real Redheads 69
I'm Waiting For   70

5: FLASHES

Parked Outside   73
Beauty and the Beast   75
Confession   76
Isle of Dolls   78

6: NOVELTY

Blue Light Reverie   83
Choo-Choo, a Case Study   145

Biography   153

1: CALL FOR LOVE

TRUE CRIME AT LITTLE YORK 1929

shrieks
wake the napping child's body
curled next to Mother

shrieks and sun motes pour in
from the country road beyond
carry the doom of rifle shots
[like fireworks]
and the sputtering-out of a Model T motor
in a moment Daddy's voice fills the bedroom—
Ed killed Gladys, then himself, in the car

[life of the July 4th farmhouse party cut short]

shrieks
enter a child's toes
shoot up her legs
tear through her gut
straight to her heart

even though her mind
knows little—
her seized-up soul cowers under Mother's
ashen face her

cold, shaking fingers

THE YEAR OF BEING THIRTEEN

August without soul,
nothing moves
sap not rising
dusty branch
crackling leaf
soon to fall....

bristle of chin
thread of hair
thin of lip
corner bubbling....

He comes toward me
Hold still he says
wet kiss—
bristles scorch my face
Don't tell he says
nothing moves
but Grandpa

SPANISH INFLUENZA 1919

they were sick as dogs 14-yr-old Edith and Mama but
not Papa or little Bobby who was 3. After they recovered
Mama took Edith and Bobby on the train from Oklahoma City
        down to Aunt Julia's Texas ranch.
It was there on the afternoon of a tornado at least it looked like
        there might be a tornado
sky all yellow with sulphur flashes some lightning they huddled in
        the storm cellar
Edith let out an ear-splitting scream said she'd seen a rattler coiled
        on a ledge above
My, what a scream to come out of a scrawny teenaged girl
Why Edith, you must be imagining things
but it was true one of the hired hands saw it, too, said he was going
        to have a
wrestling match with the snake he reached up, Edith screamed
        again
then Aunt Julia said leave the snake alone we are going back to the
        house
Edith told Mama the snake stared at her that he had eyes like
        Papa's, always
staring at her Mama said don't be silly
Next morning Edith was in the bathhouse, saw another snake
        coiled on a ledge
went screaming naked as a jaybird into Aunt Julia's kitchen
why she still ain't got no titties, cackled someone's aged grandma
        sucking on her corncob
pipe rocking on the back porch
everybody laughed to see Edith, lanky as a winter tree, still no tits!

back home in Oklahoma City, Mama decided to take Bobby back to
        Kentucky
to show off her beautiful child to her mother and her sisters
leaving Edith alone in the house with Papa one morning he was
        standing in her bedroom
doorway looking at her as she lay under the covers
she knew what was going to happen
drew the covers up tight under her chin
didn't matter

decided she would scream bloody murder loud enough for the
            neighbors to hear
and Papa would leap from her bed undone
as though he had never been there
and that's what happened

when Mama came back from Kentucky Edith told her what Papa
            had tried to do
Mama just said "awww" and pushed the air with her open hand as
            though what can
you expect from a man like that who won't even take care of his
            family a man who stands
on the street corner all day long jawing with his cronies

but it didn't mean Edith stopped loving Papa after all he was her
            father
he'd given her a cameo ring for her 12th birthday
(where'd you get the money for that, Mama stormed)
one morning brought her a tumbler of whisky saying this'll put hair
            on your chest
Edith made a face at the smell turned on her pillow Take it away,
            Papa

STRANGE

troubled girl of 14,
I turned to Mother:
she pulled out a knife,
stabbed my shadow

I packed up my dream bag
departed for unknown destinations
heard strange voices
listened to strange music
talked to strange people
loved strange men
wrote strange stories

nothing but strange would do

it was you, Mother,
who sent me soaring
thru the twilight sky of girlhood
into the midnight blue of strange

THE VIRGIN SPRINGS

she stands at the brink
maybe now
(words of the moment)

she splashes in—
newly leafed trees from brookside
bend over her
not yet

she puddles her way to a stony ridge
parting the rippled mirror
skips from rock to slippery rock
enters a broad blazing waterway

decades of mothers spook this river
her toes curled this way
then that

full force overtakes her
she bobs up and down
gasping
along with a rush of last year's leaves
scrambling hustling seeking the edge

she leaps out
lands on a slope of new mud

not yet caught
she will hide over there
in that bed of lavender weeds
until he discovers he

INTEMPERANCE

Girl and her books
leave campus for home
6 pm she
stands in a lava flow
pulsing magma
from the beat of the Dance Studio

Southbound headlights
pick through westside winter gloom
shadow the frozen bricks
of Academe

North winds
sink her from sidewalk to subway—
in the train's hot rush and sway
fevered dreams erupt:
last summer's molten kiss consumes her

Not the ice-blue embrace
of Mother's house
in the temperate zone

ALCOHOL DOG

war is over
dizzy life begins in Daddy's town
he was the speakeasy dog in the 20s
now it's *her* turn to howl!

comes the weekend
shove the books aside
put the brain to sleep
New Years Eve yelping down Park Avenue
cab packed, party in Queens
she danced to bands Hotel Pennsylvania
hid anywhere….in burrows, in dens
Sigma Chi House top floor street floor
the *real* doghouse
midnight in Central Park
love swarmed in the grass
Little Casino in the Village
a coffee-colored man sang
Your arms opened wide to take me inside
parked in a Jersey swamp
home at dawn the cold house smoke-stale
with Daddy's Camels
Stop crying, Mother

through the web of Manhattan dreams
she found him
all warm beast eyes and tender paws
offered her a drink at twilight
Here's the hair of the dog that bit you
his favorite metaphor
(feeding her drinks since she was 10
hey, even a beer age 5)
wasn't that how all this started, Daddy….?
no different from the dogs who followed
handing her a drink….

HOW SHE ROLLS INTO HER GAME

that moment of ecstasy she gives herself
before falling asleep

it's about these women
she has known them all her life
they whisper at twilight over teacups
tell secrets in the kitchen
behind the swinging door

the older one, hair stacked in grey wieners,
laughs, stirs the gravy
eyeglasses steam up at the stove
or
bends to the sewing-machine
pumps the treadle
the younger one always watching
blue eyes like glacial stones
her smile a glare of bright fangs
across the dance studio

they have been with her since she was born

harsh streets where these women lived
shop and office where they worked
then *she* came along

now...
when they need money
the women strip off her showgirl costumes
the ones they've measured her for
pinned her up in
glitter of rhinestones
sheen of satin
velvet moss
all thrown in a heap on the floor
tie her half-naked to a wheel
splay her out
invite men in

AUGUST HER WAR 1944

holding close to her breast
mean-patched jowls of the city
lush stink of sidewalk
hard as August cement
rusty as chrome fenders
humidity bears down
imminent as a double-decker bus
pounding Fifth Avenue
in heavy weather

office doorknobs
clang of monitor bells
clacking typewriter keys
wounded women sturdy as desks
bandaged in black
their men at Anzio
howl "Dirty Gerty from Bizerte"
in mud-crusted heat and sweat

sixteen summers and now her war
whirling white her free-swing skirt
the time of high heels
thigh-gartered nylons
holding her sailor's hand
his middy blouse cast to the far Pacific
Leyte and New Caledonia
1944 his bell bottom letters
dark ribbons of hope
twine her heart

smoke and litter
hot winds
swell from the W. 23rd Street subway stop—
the train grinds, squeals
halts in deadly dust

PURSUIT ON W. 115TH STREET

It wasn't the first time
you lay down for me, Don
nor the last

your strange torpor....

in that corner room of yours
we sometimes practiced sorcery for hours
        (eye of worm
         moon of Mercury)
drawn shade
baked yellow by sun
throbbing light
heated the room to hyperbole
music was there
        (you beat the tambourine
        I blew the penny-whistle)
terror and pain, too

no matter how many times
I knocked on your door
no matter how many times
you let me in—
well....

you danced with men? was that it?

that building on 115th Street
was demolished years ago
you died an old man, Don
somewhere else

REVLON CALL FOR LOVE

pink angora sweater fuzzy soft
tight along her breasts
walks down Main Street
past vacant storefronts
pink as a baby cloud floating
lipstick Revlon purple pink
tiny toes like bald rodents
wriggling bare Super Lustrous
the polished tips Nipple Pink new Siren tricks
Vagina Rose Revlon's deepest shade

she's pink as pink can be
virgin thighs a call for love
swaying across the railroad bridge
wrap those Lustrous lips around this, he says
from a dark doorway
save her the best shot,
Money Shot,
Revlon's most alluring fragrance,
more potent than Flair or She or Downtown Girl
turns your spit and semen fuchsia pink

walks down Main Street
hugging herself in the pleasure of it
the looks the whistles the hands
the call to arms
Revlon Punk the new shade
wrap those Revlon lips around this
he says motioning her
she could comply
at a doorway
to kneel between his, if she thinks about it,
outstretched legs

AMSTERDAM AVENUE 1949

you on the curb of dirt-scabbed streets
crumbled, streaked
mold this into unborn eyes
steps to a divine cathedral
scaffolding where Uncle Bob fell as a kid
scarred his chin for life

scratch 'what is love' on the wooden john door
count dark bricks bedded in concrete
your body swollen with flower
seeded, now about to burst
sway in elevators, corridors grout-grimed
sniff cabbage and onions
balance the tilt of dumbwaiters
at the door Harold buttons up his fly
drop into mouse holes
rotten egg—run for your life

Nat fathering your womb
this wasn't love, was it?
he races slips of paper
into canopied candy stores
for Pinky the bookie

belly drop that morning
is your heart big enough to hold it all?

Ruth types the words
cigarettes smoke her crowded corner office
at her window Columbia rears monstrous
the lion greedy in its den
trucks and buses rumble by

count the hours night and day
among the garbage pails
short walk to the hospital
you were born there, too, weren't you?
didn't Daddy call you 'Sprout'?

single weed bends from a sidewalk crack
dirt scabs patched up, perfect bloom of a baby
new decade sprouting—she mewls in the night

2: HOW SHE ROLLS

JESSICA AT CAPE MAY 2002

hipshot she stands
pillar of cream her passion
beach of sand and seagrass
rims her skin
she dreams herself into the boy
left him behind for a moment
longs for him already
hot cream and hipshot
buoyant and fast running
waves rush her,
surf sunshot with its own fever

RIDDLE ME

twilight comes soft, opaque
you have to climb through it,
shreds of cloud trail.
She tries to explain
I know what happens
but I don't know why

deep along the dream
comes a melodrama
that no one talks about.
She says
who would understand mine
anyway?
no sharing here
it's a ritual road
tracks carved in solitude
more like an old furrow
plowed many times
where streams converge
starts with a trickle
ends in a waterfall.

She adds with a sad smile
I meet strangers there
and dead lovers
they welcome me
I help them by being docile
we exchange a few words
mostly we're silent
when we're done
the dam broken
I come up for air
you'd never guess
where I've been
what's been done to me

PORN STAR

Candi Cone—where
did you ever get that name?
just because you were baptized Candace?
pretty little girl of the Bronx
dancing and dreaming
like any other good little girl
daddy a jazz musician
mommy left early on
a cruel stepmother
(or maybe only frightened)
what you saw in your bedroom at night
daddy and your older sister
swallow the shame...still

it helped you make it to the big time
heroin and coke made it easy, too,
so did the Mitchell Brothers
famous in San Francisco
and New York
in cafés, men stop and stare at you
they've seen you in their best dreams
and on film
the forbidden kind

now you're sleek and sixty
directing, producing
nice porn films for ladies
to educate them, Candi Cone

SHAPE OF FRED HAINES (1936-2008)

tales of your pale-haired groin
lit up a thousand smoky flights

Ulysses man 1967
you put Joyce onscreen
you an Oscar boy—I could well believe it

and all the time
at home between your Gypsy lips
a Gitane

I knew you before the Gitanes
you and your leather jacket in Berkeley
KPFA up the stairs downtown
broadcast Lenny Bruce at midnight
almost lost our license
yours and Dede's flat on Wheeler Street
(walls painted black)
chess at the Steppenwolf
staff party at Gert's
my Friday night blowout
you at the piano
black shades hid your fire blue eyes
dazzled by connection

I dreamed of trips-out in the dark
as if my earthy Fred-shaped path
could fit your jigsaw map
your traveled thighs outdistanced mine—

you left town
then I left town
my alternate route as crazed as yours

Gitanes finally got you
Venice on the Pacific
solitary cottage
lungs blackened

ABYSS

the hole kept getting bigger

she staggered out of her bedroom
down the hall to the dining room
and there, by one of the chairs,
she was stopped by the sight of the hole
spreading from where she stood
she was about to fall into it

she didn't care about her husband, only
her children
(who knew nothing about the nightmare man
at her heels)
though she could no longer see her children while
standing over their bodies in bed

to the hospital for pills
Have you been assaulted?
no...yes...I wanted it

she trembled—
Mother was reading *Bluebeard*
wives hung on hooks in the locked closet
blood pooled at their dangled feet
Mother's thready voice called up to the lookout tower:
Sister Anne, Sister Anne, do you see my brothers coming?

the pills kicked in,
she fell asleep hiding the tell tale key
(Fatima waiting for rescue)

pills
hypo
breathless she slid down a no-holds brick wall
the abyss waited below

she pretended to be alive
ghost living in a foreign land....

EXPLANATION FOR THE MAN STILL WAITING AT THE CORNER

On a decayed place I stumbled
[a street turned savage through hard times…shots heard in the
        distance]
finding *you* there with a chalice of burning liquid
thirsty I drank your dark face
long nights at the Grail ensued
        [she became someone else
        designs of the cracked ceiling her new map of the world
                billboard astride the Port of Oakland
                flashed the Year of Our Lord 1962….
        on her back, aflame under his ministrations
        and the walls echoed *baby baby baby*
        swarm of alien bees engorged her soul]
you spoke of your life
I reveled in its martyrdom
desperate master
I pleaded for more
to give myself up to your crucified city
melt my bones into its spiked streets
forsake my own life to live out more of yours
that spiraled across me—

        and

        [when the last bell tolled
        she knew she couldn't
        follow him]

        down

TANGOMASTER

her patent leather heel spikes his ankle
the portly man in black suit and white shirt
jerks her thru the alley

a silk scarf covers his wattles
aging fat man lithe as a snake
desire still potent

she takes it
she takes it all
the press of his hand on her back
the turn of his lofty thigh
the grip on her gut

she takes the hard pull
it rips her apart
brava the torn dress
the mad tongue
the dark heart
pushes her to the stony plaza
to the rise and fall of accordions
the soaring street singers
to the circle of gasping onlookers
they cheer her pliant swoon
dazed eyes

RED HOT

it was still morning
and he began to burn
in a room of many windows
looking out on a side street of the city

watched her with those shoes
she was barefoot in jeans
and a flowered pajama top
flowers red as a cat's tongue
as though she had just hopped out of bed
husband a minus since dawn
they were gold spike-heeled sandals
she held them in her lap
played with the straps
as she might play with any man
her hands small, fingers tender soft

in the room a brown leather couch
an upright piano, stool to whirl
a TV set on a bench
a chair upholstered green
where he chose to sit
after she answered the door
and invited him in

she took in his rap
from a deeper chair
where she nestled careless
her scorched honey hair kicking back
across the cushion
turned toward him, gave him the once-over
he began to burn

it would happen that night
they would meet on a corner
the flowers on her pajama top still red
red as a cat's tongue, that's what she was
a kitten he could throw high in the air

catch in his arms when she fell,
and he would explore her
find her parts as hot as a killer's tongue
pulsing blood-red as last night's sunset

HIGH TIMES ON FILLMORE STREET 1968

poor Bobby had a bullet in his thigh
he wouldn't tell me who had put it there
we lit up joints to reach a mellow high
then danced till dawn and scarcely had a care

he wouldn't tell me who had put it there
his girlfriend's flat was soon filled up with folks
we danced till dawn and scarcely had a care
we never had a shortage of shared tokes

his girlfriend's flat was soon filled up with folks
I hoped this night would never have an end
we never had a shortage of shared tokes
to leave at dawn would on a cab depend

I hoped this night would never have an end
but Clarence had the money so we left
to leave at dawn would on a cab depend
I mourned for Bobby; and I felt bereft

but Clarence had the money so we left
poor Bobby had a bullet in his thigh
I mourned for Bobby, and I felt bereft
we shared a final joint and said goodbye

DAWN AND DIRTY

sunrise
here I am filthy
from the worm holes
that housed me during the night
we hold our breath
in the tunnel of your bed
lip to lip
limb to limb
as she knocks I am forbidden to breathe
or make a sound
she keeps knocking, calling out

slipshod through crackling subways
breast exposed to the roil of the strap hanging crowd
your hand at my mouth
your body suffocating mine
while he thrashes her under and over
unwieldy wooden turnstiles
ironworks where squealing wheels
jut in and out of grout-grained stations
always seeking a home
she looks to you for comfort
poor baby she's been laid up for weeks
beaten silly by her movie star husband
lying drunk on the rat tracks with his new mistress

she keeps knocking
whining and squalling like wind
blown into the grime of early light
my earrings that I left on the tiles
never saw them again after that night
when I held my breath as a favor to you
which girlfriend did you give them to?

not that I cared
groping around down here
slow climb to the El
rusted rails to morning

ROCK ME

skyscraper daddy I call you
my hyperbolic New York pal
built on the phallic principle
stable as bedrock
winsome as the Waldorf
rock and rush
rock me, daddy
let me hug you
I'm a building-hugger
tall as a tree
thick as Grant's Tomb
brutish as the Brooklyn Bridge
squeeze me, won't you?
your hair slick as tar
lips wet as rainy streets
ply me at the Plaza
your stump strains…
stand up for me
no falling down
like the Twins, those wimps!
swing me onto your saddle
slip me into your subway
liberate me at the Library
tail me in your taxi
hump me in the Hudson
crazy gone as the Astor Bar
juggle me daddy
diddle me silly
under your lunatic lamppost
down Fifth, up Madison
boost me at the ballet
frisk me at the Fraunces
cradle me at Columbia
ball me in Bryant Park
beat me daddy 8 to the bar

SOFTLY PURRING HE RAPES HER PURSE

King of Cats
denizen of dark alleys
muscled, sleek and smiling
whiskers angled
ears on edge
slides over the back fence
six pack under his arm
out of Lisa's yard
into Megan's

Surprise!

scratches at the door
purrs her name whatever it is—confusion
after a day at the track
lost a bundle
but what of it?
he knows where to pounce....

Claws retracted
his velvet paws
massage her fur
into oblivion—
she'll forget she ever had a purse
Mmmmmmeow!

3: STRANGE NIGHTS

SUMMER NIGHT SWIM

in the stone quarry flooded
you and I hot as July
shallow the moon glitter
toes paled, lips silvered
metallic glaze on a gushing plain
voices a net of echoes
ears silenced we leave the others
sink through the midnight pool
rocky nip of boulders
fevered jut of flesh
how we grow under the press of fingers
caress of dreams in a bowl of water
cool
lapping at arms and legs
your arms and legs
wrapping me at the flood

JUST FOR A MINUTE

he said
I want to go inside you
        just for a minute
        just to get the feel of you
and I said yes
so he did
        just to get the feel of me
he said I want to go inside you
        for a minute
to get the feel of you
and I said yes
        and he did
and I said I'm glad you did
and he said I wanted to
        get the feel of you
I said I know

HEIGHT

you said, I'm not very tall
I said, but you have a hard body
I once loved a man who was shorter than you
I loved him more than anything
you said, did he have a hard body
I said not as hard as yours

you bent and kissed my cheek

soon we lay in the woods
I rested my head on your chest
your feet reached beyond mine
see, I said, you're much longer than I am
you said the trees are taller than both of us
I said your arms are long, too
like branches of your body
how easily they wrap around me
you said, your body is softer than mine

I reached up and kissed you on the lips

soon your hard body
was stretched over my soft body
your lips at my lips
your legs stretched longer than mine
we lay still for awhile
leaves rustled above
sun went down, stars came out,
moon came up
you moved within me
I said I love you more than anything

OUR SHEETS ARE COOL & SMOOTH

daylight opens our bed
your voice like driveway gravel
stir of chimes in the wind
guttering leaves
squirrel-patter on the roof
early rain on hot pavement
I can smell it, taste it
your breath sweet as oranges
your arm at my neck
your arm hair tickles
your fingers burrow
my fingers play your tongue
your tongue not so rough as a cat's
your skin the color of teak
my lips on your skin

our sheets are cool and smooth
pillow deep and down
sink in
your body my wall against the day

SPELLING IT OUT

thanks, John Fogerty

hey, daddy,
look what you did
you put a spell on me
making me think it's love
the yearning, the craving
all mine
the moaning the howling
all mine

you put a spell on me
breaking me
tearing me
teeth of a wild dog
devouring me
made me stop runnin' around
foolin' around
doin' the thing that I did

you put a spell on me
cuz I'm yours it never stops
the yearning the craving
for the hands that undo me
the fingers that hustle me

you put a spell on me
the craving the yearning
the howling the moaning
your mouth at my throat
making me think it's love
teasing, cajoling
your growl pitched low
and thick with lust
grows deep inside me

spelling me
cuz I'm yours till I'm sick of you

FUNKY SUN

funk rocks me
walking the streets with you
after a rainy day

rain pounds the window
then you show up
funky sun comes out

sun goes down
house goes dark
you come to get me
sun rises

midnight finds me in the dark
watching the street for you
oh there you are
suddenly the funky sun!

some nights black as sin
I meet you at the corner
sun is shining

DESPERADOES

On the sidewalk
outside the pickup bar
she whirled around
her silk skirt ballooning
like a windpuffed umbrella
Young Dino
sleek and tough
 said *you're so hot*
(and she bought it)

they were driving through
Golden Gate Park
in his banged up Chevy
Dino showed her his gun
packed neatly into a shoulder holster
the deserted meadows
even the trees were lonely
their bleakness spread
across the curving roads

she said *I thought you were going*
to take me to a party in Oakland
I want to dance

he laughed *we'll dance at my place*
she thought of his gun
its intricate killing design
nestled close to his heart

his placc:
an underground cave
the shower in the one room
the toilet out back somewhere
he claimed his *real* place
was being redecorated
(she bought that, too)
he opened his leather jacket
there it was

a loaded midnight tool

As she pleasured him
she wondered:
Did he ever pull it out and say
this is a stickup?
She giggled and flung away,
making an earthquake in the bed;
what was high went low,
what was hard went soft;
Dino glared— ***Hey! Watchit!***

The following week
she was back home in L.A.
Dino called at 3 in the morning
waking her teenaged sons
her husband rolled over, grunted
it's probably for you
she tossed out of bed bleary....
Dino needed serious money
she said she could send
a twenty

he hung right up
she whispered to the hushed household
he thought I was rich....

ROMANCE

Rape, I want you to get the feel of it,
said the Green-Eyed Knight to his lady-in-arms
and she obeyed at 3 a.m.
bedded down at Grail Castle Hotel,
once the inn of gold-seekers,
storied of old, waters edge,
Port Camelot.

He held her
rammed against the bedstead's iron bars
head twisted round.
Hustled into her
deep, wide
too deep, too wide—

Hers was a small space skin space
soft place
linked to rose petals and nerve tendrils
trickled down the backs of her legs
locked in currents of pain
the rest of her life....

In too deep.
Was it only a 3-second nap
from all the fire pumped into her? or
from passion perverted,
its saturnine face darkly smiling
into hers?

She who-must-be-punished
—she began to wonder,
floated a cautionary sailboat
out across Reason's lake.

FRANKIE'S FRIED EELS

...in a cab
on her way to Tipitina's for jazz
she thought she saw Frankie Chenier
her once lover
running down Prytania Street...

back there with Frankie
café au lait skin sleek black hair
green eyes spatter of freckles
his sudden smile as he gazed at her nipples
Y'all so pink! all pink'n cream!

she died every night
held captive in Frankie's arms
like the city they lived in
caught between the Mississippi
and Lake Pontchartrain
in the crescent of its moonless joy

she loved the feel of Frankie's lips
firm and full and as well-defined
as the streetcar tracks
that run from St. Charles Avenue past the Circle
with its fine statue of Lee, downtown to Canal Street
tracks quietly erect in their low-lying path
along the neutral ground

watched Frankie cook, watched live eels dance
amid his long brown fingers
he sliced them in thirds as they squealed in agony
mangled them in butter with bits of scallion
some flour thrown in, wine, cognac
swamped them in mustard sauce....

A WALK THROUGH VLAD'S BUCHARESTI

Their reflective 1974 ramble down runneled roads viewed ragged Hotel Intercontinental stared down regimental green grass soldiers rifles readied for raging rabble riot rolling across the city square the Butcher's radiant rumbling black limo military parting of the blood-red sea ran under a sullen summer sky retreat to the raddled park its refuse-rimmed waters and rusted rowboat rutted the river rearwards then reeled back to the risible riddle of rotted rooms Hotel Union with an aphrodisiac bottle of Romanian red rapture on rumpled reverberating sheets 8th day of a curious American radical (wife-in-tow) who peeked behind Ceaucescu's Curtain saw reincarnated un-reformed un-repentant fourteenth century Vlad the Impaler who sucked souls in his bloody rubbled fortress facing Russia...

MURDER ON PARK AVENUE

is she sad?
hell, no
she's as sparkly as springtime out here
whatever else is going on...
she's got it all in hand
spike heeled boots and a rhinestone shirt
she just dumped her sweetie
or was it the other way 'round?
funny how her brain is a blank
all she remembers is that day he got so mad at her
he tried to throw her from his tenth floor window...

whatever...she's hard as cinders
hard as the mascara on her lashes
the Revlon nails at her fingertips
stalking past chrome and concrete
she won't let it disturb her days
she can take him or leave him
she doesn't care—
let him ball that back-door slut...

cars and chrome and concrete
glass walls and green lights
mascara and miniskirts,
nails and tails: she'll be wanton at the Waldorf
he never really loved her, did he?

brass gleaming all around
brass banisters, brass lanterns
Grand Central Station glitters
diamond of the city
she'll buy a real diamond some day
she'll be diamond-hard
hard enough to scratch a glass window
hard enough to drop-kick that old guy
limping across the street against traffic
she'd love to see him or someone else she knows
gut-squashed in the fast lane...

WE RETURN TO THAT STREET

Under my breath
in a corner of my odd-angled heart
again we leave the ghost place on W. 7th St.
we walk out to the fringe of the city
much of the long night
still left to us
the cracked sidewalks
the weedy glass-littered lots
arm in arm
your wasted bone scrapes my withered flesh
we sit at the hamburger counter, remember
how our bellies were once hot with hunger?

then back to the Pack Train Hotel
up the broad wooden staircase
its hollowed steps heave and squawk
under our clanked feet

you stand in the doorway
your sharp-jointed finger at your disappeared lips
shhhh....
before we turn into the $2 room-for-a-night
to resume our sacred rituals:
dry lick
dead stick

4: FROM MY HOTEL WINDOW ...

WHAT I SAW FROM MY HOTEL WINDOW ON MY 80TH BIRTHDAY:

an expanse of still water running deep, slow, hardly moving
(like me now)
and hidden in its depths—outrageous, secret, tumbling life
as in the note I wrote 45 years ago.
I said to him I am sitting, an exile from our love, at a window on
        48th Avenue
looking out at the Pacific
next stop—China
wishing myself a world away from the pain of having to give you
        up.
Years later, you, now a dead man
buried faraway in Alabama
you are feeling no pain.
And I feel almost none

COMIC BOOK SCENARIO

Hey you! Dracula man!
you still come to me at midnight,
haunt my dreams—my old mentor
tormenting me with advice
sucking the blood from my brain
whipping me to write like a maniac
driving me to revise revise revise
we used to stalk the college corridor together
smoke your Kools in conference

then I propositioned you
drove miles through storm and rain
getting to you
Let's go for a drink I said
You said *no,*
(wrapping your cloak of sublime chastity
about your bony shoulders)
I'm not like those other professors
I don't cheat on my wife!
subsequently....
you flapped your batwings
flew off to a teaching job
in the Middle East
never to be sighted again
and all this time
your specter has had me by the throat,
Dracula man, writer of novels,
tall and spare and dark

Question:
whyja hafta go an' kill yerself?
(I just found out)
I often wondered where you were
what you were doing
Not writing any more?

now I learn you've been dead for years
Not fair, Drac!

to go without letting me suck *you* dry

TRIANGLE

ping!
a tinny sound to it
little kids play at music
as you have played with me
while she looked on…

say, weren't you the one?
grabbed me by the tit
hurled me into the air
caught me on your pointed boot
whirled me around
hugged me tight
forced my lips into your needy neck

while she looked on…

your tail between your legs
sniffed me out
snuggled into my armpit
leered at my breast (but slyly)
kept up the front
while she looked on
mocked your puritan soul

your three-cornered hat
thrown down in the grass
mad matador faces an addled cow
out to pasture feeding slowly
ruminates on her milky past
rethinks her lineup of well-hung bulls

the pasture now *your* stadium
your wife the jeering crowd
I fall back, tired of
waiting for the prick of your lance
hear her triumphant *ho ho*
from the nearby stands

let me tell you something, sonny—
I never really wanted you
anyway

SOLDIER

down the years
I looked for you everywhere
in London walking the Strand
I thought I felt your heartbeat under my feet
in Paris on the Rue Madame
awakened at midnight by a car alarm
was that you signaling me?

I looked in museums
saw a portrait that was you
and in restaurants the menu
spelled out your favorite ribeye
trattorias and cafés, bierstubs in Dresden
the train station in Sofia
you sat on your luggage waiting for me
under the oaks in New Orleans
you called me from the Columns
hurricane whipping the phone wires
your voice lost in the wind

everywhere
I, the old lady, searched
for the ghost of a broken romance

our kiss in the shadows
of the long-gone Astor Bar
still lingers on my lips

and

after all this time,
where did I find you?
in a graveyard in Virginia
burial ground of soldiers—
you'd been hiding from me
prone, flat, dead in the hole
the one they dug for you 40 years ago—

TAKE A VACATION

ask her
she was married to it
wise guys straight off the street
110th by Broadway
swarm to Belmont
place their bets
laugh in their beer
take a vacation
how many bodies in the Hudson?

she didn't just sit there
o no!
she had her own game
take a vacation
dawn came up dirty
sweating too hot in the motel room
hey! turn down the heat
what the fuck! Dino!
"I cried like a baby"…

murder with a smile
life in a rush, take a vacation
all paid for
shot in his L.A. pool
Jack M, mafito from Sheepshead Bay
his girlfriend survived
Chuck B sent up for grand theft auto

dead voice on the phone—Norman at midnight
Nick there?
carrying porn tapes to the junkyard
dogs bark
take a vacation
Miami Beach
Merry Xmas, Mom

LIKE AN IDIOT...

I followed him to Boston on the train
Although he didn't know it at the time
I saw him kiss a woman in the rain
I understood the reason and the rhyme.

Although he didn't know it at the time
I'd feared another woman in his heart
I understood the reason and the rhyme
I guess our love was doomed right from the start.

I'd feared another woman in his heart
Someone he'd known from many years ago
I guess our love was doomed right from the start
I wept to see their kiss was long and slow.

Someone he'd known from many years ago
Would now the mistress of his thoughts remain
I wept to see their kiss was long and slow
I followed him to Boston on the train.

PENTHOUSE MAGAZINE IN AFGHANISTAN

Joy unconfined! in a world of Hell—

for men under enemy fire
we're here for you
we wenches of war
proud of our brazen boobs
honored to join you
on the battleground of love

We come in all shapes and shades
amber cream and honey
check out
our fuck-me heels
jacked-up calves
bivalve hips
high end butts
hairless lips…

welded together
airbrushed
                to make your base
                a prettier place
cruise us
use us
we're your Bagram baggage
(flown-in)
Heaven-sent technology
for dreamland combat

FREE FALL TO LOVE

warm water plunge
Domina, the whale shark—
her free fall
to the sea floor
one mile down she goes
then upsurge
warm water
surge through
plunge
open mouth
surge of plankton
free fall
warm water and a caress
free fall to love
her belly cradling 100s of eggs
majesty of pupping
mystery and majesty
pupping and plunge
surge of love this pupping
plunge of Domina
warm water Domina

MEMORY OF MY DANCER

pressed tight against your orchid
sienna in your skin
glint of tango in your eye
Argentina on your tongue
gleam of moonlight on your brow
other dancers pushed us closer
barely moving
dizzy in your heated hills
we climbed the peak
shaking underground
my earthquake house
slanting floor
open door

MY DOG IS NOW MY LOVER

old lady all dried up
bent over
knees knocking, belly sagging
hair grizzled
teeth snaggled
nerves frazzled
Who would want me?

Except Digger my German Shepherd
he lieth beside me at night
he restoreth my soul
he leadeth me beside still waters

Yes, it's Digger, my faithful prince
sprawled next to me on the bed
watching TV
sharing a bowl of Cheesits

Digger! of the long lean well-muscled body
eyes like brown soup
wet black muzzle nosing out my misery
pawing me for one more Cheesit
Digger wants me!

REAL REDHEADS

Grandma was a redhead
I never met her she lived so long ago
she was a brave redhead with ten kids
captured by the Brits in 1780
dragged to a Wyandotte village
lived only to 53
died of 'dropsy'
says so in the family Bible
I revere her...

doesn't say anywhere that she was a redhead
but I know it; story's been handed down
Grandpa was a redhead, too, six foot five
big scary giant of a man
staring bright blue eyes
lived to be 90

their kids were all redheads
that's what I'm told
it's probably true
even if I'm a lying bitch of a poet

I'M WAITING FOR

sitting here waiting for the
waiting for the news
waiting for the news of
your death

waiting for the hiccup
the sneeze
for the turn of a card
roll of dice
end of race
phone call
mood change

wait for the wave
to the shore
the leaf in its fall
for what you said
it will happen, you said
mournfully
not tonight but soon
I'll do it, you said
wait for the

5: FLASHES

PARKED OUTSIDE

Bernie's green Honda sits outside his apartment building not that she wants to see him—

slow, how slow it had been, sitting on the side of the bed, kiss, he interrupted her loneliness, open the bottle, pour, no rush, have a cigarette, light mine, light yours, flicker of match, maybe she'd go upstairs after all, same as that trembling staircase at the Pack Train Hotel on 7th Street where they used to go...she feels herself growing smaller and smaller until she's not herself but that figure in the far distance, that small woman in satin hot pants and spike heels sitting on the edge of the bed with Bernie, sipping Jim Beam, their first time together years ago then her clothes are off and Bernie is stacking them neatly on the chair...cars keep going past her people getting on with their lives as she sits there idling, like the motor of a beset car about to stall...

maybe now she'll quit staring at his green car, leave her own car where she's parked on the other side of the street, maybe she'll go into the lobby and ring the bell under his mailbox...they must have mailboxes in the lobby...it looks like a normal apartment house...

other cars are going by now, whishing by her like a whale's tail splashing the ocean, splashing some little puddle at her door, and there's a tiny moon up above, too, she's staring at the moon, thinking how moony white it is, wondering when it will set, the moon sets just like the sun only it's deep night now, what would Bernie be doing up there in his apartment

he'd be drinking now, glad to see her, glad to go into her, or he'd want her to sleep with Walter, if Walter were still around, want her to buy a hooker for a threesome, how much is that? another car goes by, these people driving their cars so fast, all have somewhere to go, they don't sit around in their cars trying to figure out something, Bernie reaching for her, hoping Walter was watching...she'd seen him go home to Audria, drunk on his feet, dark man bending low...tears in his eyes...everything is never enough

she could go in and he might kill her while drunk, throw her out the window, a car would drive past and no one would even notice her falling body, not knowing what he was doing, Bernie might trap her in his apartment, nobody around to keep track of him...he said he used to lie on the floor of the living room, drunk, while his kids scooped up the change that fell from his pants pocket...Audria threw him out, sick of his drinking...better than shooting up? but not much different, always nodding off, have to have another fix, whether booze or the white stuff

she pulls out of her parking space and heads for home, the green Honda dwindles into the distance of her rear view mirror and another car rushes past

BEAUTY AND THE BEAST

There was an old woman she was dancing and dancing in a big ballroom with a boy named Billy she'd dated in high school or was it the old man Chuck who had recently befriended her [both men were rather slightly built] they were dancing and dancing she said to him, 'we've never danced together before' and then a young girl came up to her and said 'your black slacks are pulled down in back we can see your white underpants' so the old woman left her partner and left the ballroom and ran upstairs to her room and saw the elastic had broken on her slacks and she put on another pair of black slacks and then, going back down the stairs, saw she was wearing bright red satin long-legged underpants and when she got downstairs to the outdoors her partner was nowhere in sight and she had to go down another flight of steps on a cliffside and when she got to the bottom, she turned and looked and saw a gorilla was coming down the stairs after her, following her she was frightened and started running along the path by the cliff but pretty soon she heard the gorilla singing *Night and day, you are the one, only you and you alone under the sun whether near to me or far it's no matter, darling, where you are, I think of you, night and day*....he had a beautiful voice; the song made her sad and she turned around and he was holding the gorilla head in his arm; she smiled and he smiled—he was a nice-looking older man—and she thanked him.

CONFESSION

All on a golden California afternoon in 1972, Girard and Bascom and Polly sit in Bascom's living room. Polly's dress is short and shows off her legs in their shimmering nylons clear up to her high upper thighs. Girard and Bascom are looking at her well shaped legs. Then they look at each other and smile. Bascom is a plain looking black man with a small moustache and slight features, slight body. Girard has a stunning physical presence, tall, slim, muscular, the café au lait of his face spattered with freckles, eyes green, hair sleek and black and curling a little, lips thick and well-defined.

Bascom sits now, looking at Polly's legs, returning Girard's wink. He tells them how he used to be a driver for a black gangster in Houston. Then he tells some story of how he was in charge of the panties of the gangster's girlfriend. Polly wonders, did he inspect them after they were worn by the girlfriend? Act as a panty spy? Girard enjoys these stories. He has a rich, deep laugh. As he drinks Bascom's bourbon, or maybe it's the bourbon Polly thoughtfully brought with her for the afternoon's drinking, Girard lapses more and more into ghetto dialect so that Polly can hardly understand what he's saying.

The gold of the afternoon is beginning to fade. Polly has to get home with the big convertible her husband Nicholas has lent her. Although a university professor, he's also a self-styled "car jockey" working for an insurance crook in L.A. who, as a sideline, delivers people's cars cross country for them when they don't want to drive the cars themselves. The mileage on the odometers of these cars is usually turned back so the owners won't know Polly's husband has been using them for his own purposes. This afternoon, Polly used this car instead of her own small Volvo to pick up Bascom and Girard at work in the cannery and bring them back to Bascom's house in Oakland. Like Polly, Girard has a family waiting at home for him in Berkeley. At the end of this golden afternoon, she'll drive Girard into Berkeley, dropping him off a block from his house.

But first Girard and Polly will go into Bascom's bedroom while Bascom remains in his living room drinking, sitting where he can have a clear view of Polly undressing in the bedroom. She knows Girard wants her to sleep with Bascom.

"Did he see you undressing?" he asks eagerly.

"No."

Girard howls with disappointment. "Why not?"

Polly shrugs and slides her small, voluptuous body into the bed with him and grasps his long, golden rod, the strongest, hardest part of him. Some day soon she will make Girard happy by fucking Bascom. But she'll do it on her own, when Girard isn't around.

It's her way of getting even with him for going back to his wife after Nicholas broke up their affair ten years before. She realizes she's being unreasonable because after all, neither she nor Girard were ready to leave their families to live in some dump on West 7th Street near the Port of Oakland. Still, she's never gotten over the Girard of the early 60s and their delirious nights together at the Pack Train Hotel. Yet when her mind is present in her real world, she resents constantly lending him money now for booze. And recently, he's wanted her to hire a hooker so they can have a threesome, as though she weren't enough for him. At their house in the Berkeley hills, Polly finds her husband returned from the racetrack, sitting in their newly-painted kitchen drinking beer and watching baseball on the small set on the still-glistening, paint-sleek counter. He looks at her when she asks, "Is the paint dry?" He shrugs, probably wondering where she's been. Or maybe not.

ISLE OF DOLLS

I'm finally on my way down to St. Peter St. to see Tante Leopoldine, otherwise known as the Polders, named after some distant Belgian king in the chaotic woodpile of her genealogy. The Polders runs a doll shop across from City Park and she's as dark and thin and diminutive as one of her foreign dolls. I'm remembering the little house where my mother and I used to visit her years ago, the place where she kept many of her well dressed, well cared for dolls in chairs, in high chairs, in rocking chairs, and in baby carriages, all along the main hall that ran through the middle of her shotgun cottage. We called it the Doll House. Now I'm in the Polders' shop, and this is what she has to say: *Well, where on earth have you been?...Be nice, Auntie, I'm not feeling so hot. My lover died...And he was? Someone I should know?* The Polders turns to an exquisitely dressed French doll at her side, a doll she calls Tipitina named after an uptown jazz club here in New Orleans, and to whom she murmurs incessantly. Tipitina is arrayed in shades of beige and brown silk and voile, trimmed with gilt beads and featuring a tall, cone-shaped medieval headdress trailing a long diaphanous veil. The Polders mutters to her: *She hasn't come to see me in months—her only living blood relative—Memere Coq would be shocked at the life she's been living, first one man, then another...and now she expects me to know all about her activities Not that I particularly want to know in case the cops come to question me....* The Polders pauses to let this sink in. *Then you went off to that old guy up in Georgia. Yes, and where is* **he** *now?...He died.* The Polders turns again to Tipitina. *She has the magic touch, darling. Two dead husbands in one year. How does she get away with these murders anyway?* I begin walking up and down the narrow lamplit aisles of dolls. I find it macabre to gaze into their glassy-eyed faces—the eyeballs of sparkling blue, lambent brown, mouths either smiling or pouting, baby dolls in diapers and white shirts that look like real babies fresh from nursing at powerful porcelain breasts. A rigidly carved soldier riding a rocking horse seems to beckon to me. He stares straight at me with stony black eyes, a painted black walrus mustache concealing what should be his mouth. His horse rocks slightly—for a split second. I'm tempted to confide in him. Dolls don't reveal secrets, especially not dead soldier dolls. They have too many battleground secrets already. They're like locked silent vaults.

What's inside? Nobody knows. Not even the Polders, in spite of her long acquaintanceship with dolls of all sorts.

6: NOVELTY

BLUE LIGHT REVERIE

Chapter One

She mused: *If I were going to write the story of my life—which I probably never will, (it's already 2004); if I were going to write the story of my life—I would start with* "Born in the old grey stone building of Women's Hospital sprawled across an entire city block at Amsterdam and 110th Street...." She still had a photograph of the hospital on her fancy, hospital-issued birth certificate—Francine Elise Roth. But the building had been torn down years ago. There was a smaller, uglier brick building in its place.

In the steaming July twilight a blue light flickered just in front of her eyes and then disappeared as Francine Roth walked up West 73rd Street. She often saw this blue light. She was puzzled by it, but took it to be a visual phenomenon somehow connected with the aging process. She often felt a little dizzy, a little faint when she saw the blue light twinkling in front of her. Somehow the simmering color of the blue light reminded her that she had been considering using the last money on one of her credit cards to buy a blue topaz ring set in white gold that she had recently seen in Tiffany's window. She was thinking how well the blue of the ring would contrast with the ink blue color of the new silk $1,300 Gucci dress that had come into the Cranbridge Hotel shop in one of its Fall shipments that morning. Deep in her heart—those depths that she seldom dared probe—was the knowledge that she would never have the money for ring *or* dress. Blue light or no blue light, at age 68, she was lucky to have any job at all.

As she felt her walk slowing inadvertently—something seemed wrong with her right knee—she hoped she wasn't joining that tribe of arthritic older people she frequently saw tottering along the street as they pushed their grocery carts to the corner market. Or was the blue light more problematical?

It was said that in the old days Great-Grandpa Zimmer kept a blue light beaming at the door of his Raines

Law Hotel....Perhaps a red light would have made it too obvious about what was going on inside....

Francine passed the dark Gothic pile of the Dakota, a remnant of the old days, vaguely thankful that she had survived another ride on the subway, without being blown to bits by a Nirvana-seeking terrorist who had been told he would meet 75 virgins "up there". She crossed 73rd Street to the side where a row of brownstones still stood. Like the Dakota, these had also been here a long time.

The last sun rays glittered on the gold epaulets of the uniformed doorman at her apartment building—the Park Royale—as he smilingly greeted her—his dark face gleaming with good will—and opened the door for her. *Thanks, Philip...My pleasure, madam.* He bent toward her almost as though he planned to kiss her. Philip had once told her he was a part-time minister in Brooklyn. *My god, he had to come all the way from Brooklyn every day just for this lousy job!*

The blue light persisted as she strode across the lobby. *She is bending over Percie's hospital bed where he lies with his eyes closed, features inert. She tells him she has a secret.* I have a secret, Percie. Many secrets. It's important that I tell you this. I have never told anyone else. *Percie does not respond. Francine clamps her hand on his forehead. It's hot and sweaty. A rank aroma rises from his body. She hears footsteps coming down the cold white hospital corridor, the dismal hall made narrower by empty gurneys and piles of medical supplies set against the white walls. The nurse comes in to check his life support system—wires and cords, the bags to catch his effluvia, bottles hung upside down, the monitor flashing and spinning. Percie's mouth drops open. He begins to snore loudly. The nurse turns on Francine, asking her pointedly if she's been "messing with the equipment". She adds that Percie is "going fast". Francine speaks again.* Percie, I have a secret...*Bending over Percie with a stethoscope, the nurse speaks sharply.* You'd better wait out in the hall. I have to get the doctor here. *The death rattle...That was the end of Percie. His face, that had just previously been flushed a brilliant pink as though he were extremely drunk, a way Francine had seen it many times, was now turning black.* At times, she thought perhaps she had already told him her secret after all and that this was what had killed him. But then, the survivors always feel guilty, somehow responsible for the death of a loved one.

A hot shudder of cold terror jolted Francine's body when she realized Percie was dead. She had neglected her own son in her lifelong pursuit of Percie!

Francine is 68. The walk from the subway on Central Park West to her studio in the Park Royale signals the end of her day at the Cranbridge Hotel's elegant dress shop at 64th and Lex, operated largely for its tourist clientele, and the beginning of night, Francine's favorite time. After the grueling work hours under boss Polly's imperious eye, helping matrons try on dresses too young, too small, too outrageously "designer" for their outsized, drooping bodies; and after the drab, grinding subway ride uptown, Francine loves the luxurious lobby of the Park Royale with its Persian rugs, deep velour club chairs and an all-powerful, blazing chandelier. She touches her delicate chandelier earrings, feeling the rhinestones and intricate coral beading, that she wears with her midnight blue slacks and grey silk t-shirt to make herself feel more luxurious and somehow longer in height. Why does she have to be so short?

At 68, Francine Roth now wants all the luxury she can get. She thinks she might fly to Dubai, a city of sin and unqualified luxury in the Arab Emirates—noisy bars, jazzy dancing palaces, quietly palpitating casinos, all the places Francine fervently craves. But she figures she's too old to make such an outlandish and potentially dangerous trip, although she shouldn't be worried about dying—she probably doesn't have too many years left to her anyway. But she doesn't want to die horribly. Weren't some of the 9/11 suicide bombers from Dubai? Or somewhere. She tries not to think of war and politics. The vulnerable city she lives in is bad enough. Very bad news since the twin towers went down. And little help from the government. Too depressing.

Francine wants to be young again, feeling safe and just having fun. The way it was with her twin cousins Percie and Christian, Percie short for King Arthur's Percival, the shy dreamer who sought the Holy Grail, cousin Percie now lying in a four-part grave at Green-Wood Cemetery in

Brooklyn. Arranged somehow around him are Francine's father Charles "Chick" Roth and two of the Stolzenbergers, of the funeral home family Francine's great-grandmother had married into after her first husband Roth had died....mysteriously. Francine thinks of the gravesite as the "four-plex" and she cherishes it immensely, mainly because Percie and Daddy are there, blood relatives, though now bloodless courtesy the embalmer.

When she visits the grave, which she manages to do about twice a year, she whispers *I love you, I love you* to them over and over. And when she herself dies, she wants it to be in a nice clean hospital bed with a morphine drip attached to her arm, just like Percie, and then to have her ashes interred in the "four-plex" at Green-Wood.

To get to Green-Wood, she has to take a taxi from Manhattan. It's expensive.

Then there is Bobo Jennings. If anything happened to Marjorie, Francine knows she would step in to take care of Bobo. Because if it weren't for her old friend Bobo...They have known each other since babyhood when both their families occupied those grand old apartment buildings in the northwestern regions of the city bordering the Hudson—Inwood at the northern tip of Manhattan, and Kingsbridge, southeast Bronx, the Bronx that was once Bronk's Landing. If not for Bobo, she wouldn't have a place to live. She is exactly 21 months older than Bobo. Poor man, he is now crippled by a fall twenty years ago in the bathtub in Alaska, a fall so bad he was knocked into a coma for a month and had to learn to walk and talk all over again.

Francine suspects drugs played a part in it. Years ago he had been scornful of her polite librium addiction. The one she had put an end to once her "nervous breakdown" with its accompanying panic attacks had played out. *Five milligrams? Is that all you can take at one time? That's nothing...Well, I'm kind of small, Bobo. I can't absorb the big doses of whatever you're on...* Bobo so voluble and volatile. Now he can hardly talk. Very slow, painful, painstaking. On a cane, legs not what they used to be.

It seems that just before the accident, he had secretly married his longtime co-worker at Alaska Airlines, Marjorie, a monumental Scottish woman. He had kept the news of their marriage from his aunt who had adopted him when he was 18 on the occasion of his own mother's death in a car crash. But then, after the bathtub accident, it all came out. Why the secrecy? Of course, Francine had figured out long ago that Bobo was gay. He had always had a crush on her but seemed unable to do anything about it. She felt there was some kind of connection between the secret marriage and Bobo's gayness. He and Marjorie had bought a house together in Fairbanks. They were trying to look respectable during a time when being gay was still scandalous. They loved Alaska. But all that ended after Bobo's bathtub accident. They returned to New York for needed help from relatives. There was Bobo, of course, and then there was cousin Percie.

After Percie's death Francine had been ousted by his estranged wife, the avaricious Nellie, from Percie's shack on Fire Island. *For God's sake, we were cousins!* she had shouted at Nellie in an ugly final scene in which Francine had eventually been the winner and Nellie the loser!

Bobo then came to her rescue with a condo he owned at the Park Royale. Nothing particularly fancy about it except for its spectacular green-tiled Art Deco bathroom. Bobo had intended to sell it for a nice hunk of cash but then he let Francine move in. If she could pay the $800 monthly maintenance fee, it was hers for as long as she needed it. He and Marjorie continued to live in Chatham, New York, where they had bought wooded acreage in the foothills of the Berkshires, their house at the end of a dirt trail called Macedonia Road with a large swimmable pond at the edge of a wide swath of green lawn.

Bobo explained that they rarely stayed overnight in the city any more. If they did, they would just as soon go to a hotel.

Or...

Francine could have gone back to California. She had a lot of friends there as well as her son Larry and her ex-husband, Ray, with whom she tried to maintain close contact because, after all these years, Ray still sends her a small monthly stipend. That and her own Social Security check that is based on Ray's Social Security as well as her part-time salary at the hotel boutique are all she has to keep her going. She wants her life to continue marching forward. Ray is married to someone else now, a nice solid woman who keeps to the comforting domestic rituals Ray never had with Francine. Ray…who had once told her she was as sweet as the Rosenkavalier waltz and as sensual as Ravel's *Bolero*. Ray the Ridiculous, long, lean, untidy, with lank hair flopping across his forehead, she had hated his long, pointed penis on sight. He thought that all her yearning unhappiness could be carpeted over with a joke. Her studied involvement with him had been a self-shattering death wish. Her whole involvement with California had been a series of mis-steps, from trying to get into the movies because some guy coming on to her at a party had told her she was beautiful, to trying to write music with another would-be lover.

And Francine, moving back to New York from California, has taken back her maiden name. She's almost forgotten what her married name was. The Roths are an old New York family, stretching back, one way or another, into the past two centuries of the city. She's proud of them, spurious though their doings might be.

Life marching forward now. At this moment, greeting Philip the doorman who smilingly ushers her into the building and then moving past the Puerto Rican concierge who is sorting mail. He shakes his head at her inquiring look—no mail for you, Senorita (he likes to tease her with his heritage). She takes the elevator to the third floor.

Her studio is at the end of the wide Art Deco style hall with its mirrors, frost-shaded lights, and small bunches of fresh flowers on jutting wall shelves. It's a pleasant walk, not like walking down those narrow grey corridors where some of her friends now lived, in the newer concrete buildings with heavily forbidding steel doors that make you feel you're walking through your cellblock to a cramped 6x8 prison space.

Francine's son Larry had been in jail once—for civil disobedience, picketing a nuclear lab in Livermore, California, and then refusing to leave when the cops took over. They had arrested him for civil disobedience and taken him to Santa Rita Prison where he told Francine he was terrified the whole time. There were six others in his cell, most of them up on drug charges. Larry had slept under a table, pleading with Fate not to let him be knifed or raped. Larry so sweet, so earnest, so conscientious.

Oh, and Larry had left a message on her answering machine. She'd have to get back to him…soon. Poor Larry, she hadn't been much of a mother to him. He'd always been Ray's boy—the sports, the games, the golf, the baseball—Ray's boy. But solid. She felt she could trust Larry to do the right thing. Not much of the Roths in him.

Francine thought of her own exciting past, her late teens, caring nothing about politics or making other people happy: Dancing at the Roosevelt Grill, the Taft Grill, the Hotel Pennsylvania, to the big bands. Listening to the handsome black man at the Little Casino in the Village, the first time she heard the song *Tenderly—your arms opened wide, to take me inside*. Francine was pretty sure that's the way it went. And her date—she had forgotten his name—told her it was rumored the singer was the kept man of a French countess who had set him up in this MacDougal Street club. Getting drunk, she stared at herself in the tiny ladies' room mirror. Her hazel eyes had turned a brilliant green, emerald green. She thought she might get a tight green sweater to match the new color of her eyes. *Wouldn't she be a knockout!*

Later, parked on a deserted street, she had tried in vain for hours to bring her date to a climax. Finally giving up, she had arrived at 5 in the morning at her parents' Inwood apartment where she was still reluctantly living while attending Hunter College, waiting to find a rich man who was also good in bed, Percie now being passively engaged to that bitch Nellie, a stuck-up Vassar graduate, whom Francine had privately dubbed "the Eagle" because of her small dark darting eyes.

Entering Mom and Daddy's bedroom to apologize for the late hour, she found Mom crying for her wayward teenaged daughter. Daddy merely looked annoyed at having his sleep disturbed with all the melodrama. It was Mom's fault, wasn't it, always worrying about Francine's sex life. *Murder, she says!* But the person she felt like murdering was not Mom but her impotent date who had the nerve to write to her from Tulane a month later that *unfortunately we're sexually incompatible.* Francine was convinced she wasn't sexually incompatible with anyone. The jerk was probably a virgin.

She would now give anything to be lying in bed with Percie and Christian again, up on the screened-in sleeping porch in Greenwich where they usually spent the summer with other Roth relatives. *I have a secret, Percie.*

Fooling around in bed with her cousins up on the sleeping porch and eventually having intercourse with both of them was a secret, too. Looking back, it was hard to believe their parents weren't aware of their sexual activities, especially Mom who passionately believed a woman must remain a virgin until her wedding night. But then, Mom and Daddy usually spent the evening with the other Roths, the rich Roths, at nearby Indian Harbor Yacht Club, Mom probably too crazy with drink to think of anything but music and dancing and whether Daddy was flirting with another woman. Mom said the women always lined up to dance with Daddy. Proud, but jealous she was. *What a great dancer your father is!*

It was summertime in Greenwich. Christian, the bolder of the twins, had come to bed with a flashlight from Uncle Henry's tool chest in the basement (for under-the-covers roaming and groping) and a couple of condoms from Uncle Henry's night table. Their nightly sex games, she the pallid, unfledged body sandwiched between the eager flesh of her two boy cousins—Christian the aggressor with his bullet head and bristly black crew cut, Percie the easy-going, blond, tumescent one. Just thinking about them as young men could still give her a thrill.

In her third floor Park Royale studio and against guttering twilight, Francine pulled down the shade of the single back window that overlooked someone's colorful roof garden of potted flowers. Her studio was bare except for the futon and the broad table that held her computer. She threw off her clothes, hurling them into the cramped walk-in closet, turned on the window A/C, and stood before it allowing delicious waves of cold air to engulf her sweating body. She sat down then at the computer.

Dear Percie... Percie might be dead but she was going to communicate with him anyway. He'd always gotten a kick out of her fantasies so why stop telling him about them now, even if he were dead. Whatever afterlife he was having, he would be drunk, drink giving him the only courage he'd ever had—poor frightened boy, except when he was on the ballfield—his stock broker ghost (one of the elder Roths had purchased a seat on the Exchange for him) lurching wild-eyed uptown from Fraunces Tavern like a huge, hungry bear all the way to the West End—the Wet End, he always called it.

Or, in reverse, he might cruise from the Tip Toe Inn, a once-speakeasy in northern Manhattan that Mom and Daddy had patronized during the '20s, all the way down to the Astor bar. But this was all in ghostly New York—with its beginnings for the Roths at least in the old Alsatian district downtown. Tip Toe didn't exist any more and neither did the Astor bar.

There were bars that Percie had been thrown out of, bars that he wasn't allowed into, bars that saw him coming a mile away and refused to have anything to do with him, bars that were old and derelict as Percie was soon to be at an early age, bars that held panhandlers like the one Percie bragged that he was, even when he had a hundred bucks in his pocket. As though he wanted to be a bum and envied those dissolute men who actually were real bums, helplessly bums through birth and condition. There were bars deteriorating like Percie, brass rails gone rusty, mirrors blighted, wooden bar panels disintegrating like Percie's innards, first his gall bladder, then his colon, then his kidneys, his liver, his heart, drink like a cancer to his organs, finally his heart—that hard-working pump that had sustained him through ballgames, catching flies 'way out in center field, batting homers into the far reaches of Baker Field.

"I've decided to be an alcoholic," Percie had said when he was 24 but no one had taken him seriously. And now Francine realized he had already become one by that time.

"It's the Stock Exchange for you, young man," his Roth elders had advised. So that he might have the pleasure of bulls and bears, of watching stocks go up, go down on an erratic elevator of commerce, crashing, burning up, a 10-million dollar day, a 10-billion dollar day, Dow Jones averages, odd lots hiding in the corner, the frantic chalkboard replaced by the neon dazzle of flashing signals whirling round and round like a mechanical molding close to the ceiling of the world, the bottom dropping out, crash and burn, in the old days, numbers in hand-jotted digits large and small, in fractions and in wholes, then later, numbers in dizzying neon disarray.

With Percie's drunkenness in mind—yes, he would be drunk even in Heaven—Francine typed in the proviso *I hope you're sober enough to read this stuff. Otherwise don't worry about it. And if by any weird chance you choose to answer me, well all I can say is, fuck me sideways.*

She arranged the scene for him, Percie, the passionate lover, not so much of women, but of film noir and its sleazily indifferent heroines. It was Percie who had told her about the sluttish real-life activities of some of these once-famous and still good-looking actresses—one, Veronica of the famous blond bang, whom he had found soliciting in a downtown bar, another, the luscious Yvonne, who had gone to bed in a casual hotel tryst with one of Percie's colleagues on the Stock Exchange. Percie needed something to get him off, in Heaven though he might now be, but probably still hopefully masturbating his small, elegant penis to fulfillment as it futilely climbed the barrel of his snow-white belly. *So here it is, Percie:*

In the night, a small, slim, dark-haired woman in her early 20s walks down a rain-slicked street. Think of me, Percie, and think of midnight on deserted West 29th Street between Madison and Park where the old Arnold Constable building still stands. The woman's raincoat collar stands stiffly about her face. A broad brimmed felt hat is pulled down over her forehead where a few errant curls explode above *her glittering eyes. One hand is in her pocket; the other holds a brick that she has picked up from a building site down the street. She turns a corner and there's her target—a big-busted woman, obviously a woman of the streets, carrying a huge purse adorned with the big, showy brass letters N and R—Nellie's initials!— and garbed in the ridiculous gaudy costume of a prostitute—a dominatrix, no doubt— never mind she might have a degree from an Ivy League college—thighs bulging against a tiny, ill-fitting skirt. She should be killed just for wearing such a getup. She seems unaware of the rain. Certainly she is unaware of the predator rapidly gaining on her. The woman with the brick is very close now. She lifts the brick high over her head and brings it down on the back of the prostitute's head, sending her to the sidewalk, splayed out in all her fatness, blood pouring from the thin skin of her cranium, helplessly immobilized for all time. The woman throws the brick into a nearby garbage can and stalks off into the night, probably a block away to the Martha Washington welfare hotel where she rents a room for $20 a night. And no one the wiser.*

Now can you guess my secret, Percie?

They had found Nellie's body on a frigid December day, Fire Island virtually deserted, "left for dead" as the newspapers put it, from a savage blow to the back of the head. That was ridiculous. If there was any savagery involved, it came from Nellie who had been up and running immediately after Francine hit her from behind with a brick, savagely screeching at Francine who was, by that time, also running back to the docks, carryon and purse flapping against each thigh respectively, running for her own life along the grey wooden boardwalks, startling the deer grazing in the sparsely-wooded plots along the way—who knows what kind of weapon Nellie might have? Percie claimed once that Nellie had attacked him with a knife in the back while he was innocently showering. *The stupid bitch almost got me that time.*

Nellie might have been dripping blood from the back of her head, but she was far from "left for dead". If she had died after Francine left, it was through no fault of Francine's, Francine who had a ferry to catch to the mainland, Francine who now had to find another place to live, Francine frantically searching for Bobo's phone number in her address book. *Help me, Bobo! I think I'm in a lot of trouble.*

Either the Fire Island cops hadn't bothered or they didn't know who Nellie's last visitor had been. And Francine hadn't even told Bobo. She reserved her choicest secrets for the dead, the fact that there was another person she wanted to exterminate—a stranger named Bob who lived next door, who sometimes played music very loudly in the early hours of the morning. She had asked him to stop it, banging on his door, yelling *Please stop that racket!* Another tenant down the hall had poked her head, all sleepy and tousled, out of her door, shrieking *What's going on? You're waking everybody up!...So are you,* Francine had muttered. Bob had turned his noise down a notch, but not enough. Francine had seethed, tossing and turning, for the rest of the night. Yes, she would like to exterminate Bob. His music often still persisted into the wee hours.

The real exterminator was now at the door, a tall black hunk of a man in a yellow jumpsuit and a bag of exotic equipment. *A great big roach has been running like crazy all over my bathroom wall...That's what I'm here for. How's the mice situation?... Haven't come back—so far...Let's take a look. Say, what are all these bricks back here behind the stove?...Just trying to stop up the mice holes...Hmmm, looks like fresh droppings. Any self-respecting mouse can get around a brick. They're very supple creatures, you know...It's the roaches I hate. I don't want one biting me in the butt while I'm sleeping.*

After he had finished whisking his tools through the apartment, behind the stove and cabinets, into the bathroom, into her walk-in closet, he left a can of Contact spray for her to use on the roaches—*this stuff works pretty well*—and departed in a flash of bright yellow and long scissors-like legs.

Francine went back to the computer and signed in on the Alsatian cookbook she had copied into it, the cookbook she had rescued from Grandma Roth's house in Fanwood. She always told people that her ancestors came from Strasbourg. But she wasn't sure of this. They could have come from Riquewihr or Colmar or Milhouse. And were they French or German? The territory, with its adjoining Lorraine, had passed between French and German hands so many times, nobody knew what nationality they were.

Well, here was a recipe for "pommes de terre alsacienne"—in other words, garlic potatoes. Francine's mouth watered as she thought of this succulent dish, butter bubbling in the fry pan, thin slivers of garlic tossed in, boiled potatoes mashed and creamed with eggs, the piquancy of nutmeg flavoring, the fresh dark green of chopped parsley. Everything was so rich in this cookbook. Grandma had explained once that it had been given to her by Great-Grandma Mary Gunther Roth (finally Stolzenberger) on the occasion of Grandma Zimmer/Roth's marriage to La Gunther's older son Carl, Grandma's distant Alsatian cousin, an event that occurred some time around 1900. (Christian the younger had died the year before—how and why Francine had never found out. But then, damn it, she'd never thought to ask.) *I wish you could have seen the wedding,* Grandma Roth told Francine. *My father loaded the bathtub with ice and champagne. Then your Daddy was born a year later. And Uncle Henry two years later. And how furious my father was when Carl and I separated sometime after that. But it was Carl's drinking and gambling. I couldn't take it. He impoverished us. We asked the children—Charles was the oldest—who they wanted to live with, their father or me, and Charles said, "I want to stay with Muvver." I moved close to Charles' and Henry's nanny Babette so she could take care of them along with her own children while I went to work. But eventually I had to put your Daddy, poor little Charles, he was only six, and little Henry who was four, in the Sheltering Arms at 123rd Street when that neighborhood was still all white—and go to work. I didn't like what Charles was learning on the streets. He hugged me once and said* Goddammit, Muvver.

I was working at Duvernoy's, a fancy French bakery on Park Avenue. Then I got fired because a customer said something nasty and I threw a brioche at her, hit her right in the head! They almost had to call an ambulance, judging by her hysterical screams. I laughed as I took off my big white apron, it came down around my ankles, too big for a shorty like me, and laughed on the trolley, and laughed all the way home to my cold water walkup on 43rd Street. My father wouldn't help me. He married again after my mother died, the saddest moment of my life, and told me to go back to my husband. Husband! My father wouldn't help me at all even though he was rich enough from his whorehouse hotel to retire at age 43.

The Sheltering Arms had been torn down years ago. But the Episcopal Church—St. Mark's? —that Francine's father had attended with brother Henry and the 50 or so other little "orphans" probably still stood nearby. The pattern of farming out one's children seemed to have started with La Gunther. She had sent ten-year-old Grandpa Carl and eight-year-old Great-Uncle Christian back to relatives in Alsace, even though they had been born in Manhattan, after she was acquitted of her husband's murder. The boys came back as adults, bearing a grand piano—Francine pictures it swinging dangerously on a hoist, both onto the ship and then later in New York harbor, off the ship. The boys returned after La Gunther had secured her second husband, her defense lawyer Henry Stolzenberger—cousin of the mortuary-owning Stolzenbergers on Stanton Street. Then Christian had died. And Grandpa Carl had married Grandma Zimmer/Roth.

As for the *pommes de terre alsaciennes* one would need potatoes, butter, eggs, garlic, parsley and nutmeg to compose the recipe. This was the part that always discouraged Francine. Things just got too complicated, too much money, too much work involved. Better to go to a German restaurant and order it. Too bad Luchow's was closed down. Fourteenth Street. Their sign still adorned the side of a brick building there. When had they gone out of business? It seemed like another life.

Luchow had been a close friend, a colleague of Francine's Great Grandfather Zimmer, the one who made his own fortune with a Raines Law "hotel" in a brownstone on Eighth Street near First Avenue—a cheap saloon/restaurant/lodging, its rooms rented out mostly to prostitutes—and then bequeathed most of his money to the Masonic home in Rockland County. Great-grandfather had been the Grand Vizier—Grand Master?—or something of the Ninth District Manhattan German Masonic Lodge.

As the daughter of a fellow-restaurateur, Grandma and Daddy and Uncle Henry had been able to get the occasional free dinner at Luchow's.

The Raines Law had ordered that food be served or at least dispensed—the origin of the free lunch—in New York City where liquor was served, an early attempt to regulate the city's rampant drunkenness. Great-Grandfather Zimmer had installed his wife as cashier and the rest of his family of three sons and a mother-in-law in a next-door brownstone. With the financial help of Mme. Albers, his wife's mother who lived in the back of the brownstone with her parrot and darling little Grandma Zimmer, eventually to be Roth, Great Grandfather Zimmer soon found himself engaged in a lucrative business, more satisfying than working as a bakery clerk, his first job after coming to New York from Baden-Baden, a German spa near the French border.

And now, thinks Francine, *the last of the line is in the poorhouse, so back to the Alsatian potatoes. Well, I guess Christian still has money but he'll never part with it. I wish I could stop thinking about my ancestors! Does this preoccupation mean that I'm soon going to be joining them? I keep getting their names all mixed up anyway.*

Or maybe her mind wasn't as good as it used to be, or maybe it had never been as good as she thought it was. The heart affected the brain and most of the Roths had bad hearts. Francine hadn't had hers checked in years. She avoided bad news wherever possible. However, it was the possibility of losing brain power that frightened her most. How would she be able to pull off a murder...or even a decent shoplift?

Another message from Larry. She'd have to get back to him. He said he was worried about her. *Give me a call, Mom.* She tried to forget all this nonsense with Percie. Still, she would just like to hear Percie play the piano one more time and sing "You Made Me Love You" with his simulated Al Jolson voice that filled Aunt Elaine's living room with love and unexpected vitality, leaning away from the piano, stretching his arms toward the keys and turning his head to give Francine a half-smile.

Still pondering Alsatian potatoes, she made her favorite sandwich for herself out of leftover mashed potatoes coated with mayonnaise and packed between two large pieces of Chicago-style Italian bread. *I love you, Percie. Come back to me.*

Chapter Two

Percie was always crying. Francine blamed it on Nellie. For all her sexy ways, Nellie probably couldn't properly satisfy Percie. He was a big man with a big belly and wide, muscular shoulders, six foot four with a huge blanched-white egg-shaped face and bald dome. His eyes were small and round and pale blue, almost albino.

Yet women loved him. It must have been his deep, gentle, soothing voice and his dreamy demeanor—a young boy who had sat on the couch at 6 o'clock in the morning and habitually watched the early morning silent logo on TV during the late '40s, humming a mysterious little melody all to himself. Even then, Francine used to wonder if her dear, sweet little cousin Percie had not been born out of his time and place. Was he "inappropriate"? So unlike his fraternal brother Christian. Christian, the dark, the silent, the surly, the uncompromising, the one who had raced out of Aunt Elaine's womb twelve minutes ahead of his sluggish brother, Percie unwillingly following Christian out of the womb. The womb where Percie had lived so dreamily for nine months was a dim, comfy place where he could bud and grow, curled up and without care, without exertion where he was fed and watered, a creamy-pink, full-bodied blossom. And all his life Percie had sought to recapture that dream, sometimes surreptitiously wrapping himself in Aunt Elaine's coat to imbibe once again the aroma of the womb that had enveloped him before birth. Sweet, sluggish baby all his life.

Even as a kid Percie had had a protruding stomach from habitually overeating and a thin yellow thatch of hair that he began losing at age 19. Aunt Elaine admitted that she had once absent-mindedly stuffed mashed banana into baby Percie's mouth until he had gagged, unprotesting. His belly made a wonderful pillow for a woman's head.

And Francine loved to see him cry. When he burst into sobs while watching some paranoid tear-jerker featuring a female victim on TV, or sitting in a movie house watching a teenage drama with its ersatz happy ending, Francine would love to watch his face crumple and grow a bright pink with uncontrollable emotion. His sobs would end in hiccups as he mopped his face with the red bandanna he carried in his pants pocket for just such occasions. *I don't know why I do that...You love to do that, you masochist...Oh stop it. Stop that Freudian stuff. It's just meant to belittle me....*

Francine remembered some strangely incomplete conversations she had had with Percie. One day he told her about an incident in a crowded subway car. He had inadvertently stepped on a woman's foot and the woman had turned on him savagely and screamed at him and could be heard even above the wheeze and scream of the train. *And so did you tell her to shut her gob?...No, but I told her off...To her face?...No, in my head as I worked my way to the other end of the car...Well, that must have been effective...For me, it was,* Percie had replied forlornly. He always seemed to be at the negative end of a rebuff. *So you always let these "rejections" as you call them, you let them sit in your brain and fester. Is that right? And then you can feel sorry for yourself...Why are you always trying analyze me? So what if I have grievances. Everyone has grievances.*

Francine was the strong one, the stoic, perhaps because she had lost her mother on and off to various mental institutions all her young life. And was always cautioned to keep it a secret. A terrible secret that she had entrusted to Percie only, and only in an attempt to relieve the twisting, turning nightmare load on her heart. She kept losing Mom to the psychiatric demons who treated her at this or that Manhattan mental ward.

Poor Mom. She thought she had married Rudolph Valentino. Daddy did look a lot like the 20s' screen idol—soft olive complexion, full, sensual lips, lambent brown eyes that Mom called "cocker spaniel eyes". Even though bald from the age of 18, Daddy had attracted women by the hordes.

All the Roth men were great lovers—yes, even third cousin Rollo Roth, once considered the champion snot-taster of New York—the Roths were great lovers, even to the point of inciting violence in the jealous women who loved them. Most of the women who had married Roths had also slept with other members of the in-law relationship. *The Roths are such great lovers,* Aunt Elaine had intoned, her eyes taking on the faraway look associated with extremely pleasant memories. And it was Rollo, the last remaining devout Catholic in the family, who told his cronies on Wall Street that it was for the love of Christ that he performed *these Goddam mercy fucks.*

Hadn't Great-Grandmother Mary Gunther Roth (labeled "La Gunther", in the *New York Sun,* supposedly because her two-syllable maiden name had more zing to it than simply "Mary Roth") murdered her husband when she found out he was cheating on her? The lawyer Henry Stolzenberger had gotten her off, claiming she was defending herself from her husband's butcher knife (he owned two butcher shops, one in the East Bronx and one in Yorkville), then married her himself. Apparently *he* wasn't afraid of her!

One of the family "bibles" treasured by the Roths was the Heptameron, one of the naughty French novels written by Margaret, the 16th century queen of Navarre. It consisted of a series of stories told from one day to the next by aristocrats taking the cure at Cauderets. *Better than the Decameron,* was the Roth verdict. Francine had dipped into it once—a fat red book falling apart at its ancient seams—with softly-drawn engravings of nude women scattered throughout. A story told on the "Seventh Day" is about a woman who gives her husband powder of cantharides to make him love her, and almost kills him. In an "Eighth Day" story, a woman at the point of death flies into such a violent temper at seeing her husband kiss her maid, that she recovers. The power of passion!

It was said that Rollo had read the Heptameron in the original medieval French. He was a giant of a man, the Snot-Taster, referred to by other members of the family as "a man of many parts" and Percie resembled him in looks. Rollo referred to Percie as "Nancy Boy" and denied there was any resemblance. At family gatherings, he used to say things like *Put your panties on, Percie, the party's getting rough.* And Percie would just sit there staring blankly into space with his usual dreamy half-smile.

Rollo seemed to think Percie's piano lessons, and Percie's subsequent ability at the piano were sure signs of being gay. Percie, on the other hand, said the only reason he had agreed to take piano lessons was because he wanted to learn how to play "The Blue Danube Waltz". That accomplished, when he wanted to stop taking lessons, Elaine had insisted he continue so that he and Christian could play duets together.

The blue light was flickering in front of her again and Francine hoped she wasn't going to faint while she was thinking of

100

Inwood Hill Park where little Grandma Roth used to take her for walks when she was a baby. Bounded on the west by the Hudson and on the north by the Spuyten Duyvil (Dutch for "Spitting Devil"), as the West End of the Hudson River was called where the Harlem River flowed into it, the park was a large wild piece of rocky, hilly countryside. It was traversed by rough, wandering paths where one could glimpse a sparkle of dark water far below, paths that dipped into ravines, dipping unexpectedly upon glacial pot-holes or upon the great tulip tree, at that time almost 250 years old. Was the tree still there or had it been uprooted, chopped down, carved into rounds of firewood? One might also stumble upon the remains of Shora-Kap-Kok, an Indian cave-village.... Some writer had commented on the park's great trees, its crumbling houses (that, thought Francine, have all crumbled away by now), its remote quietness, making it hard to accept that it was actually a part of Manhattan.

Francine wondered if it had changed since her babyhood days when Grandma Roth had taken her there, taking chances, taking risks....*This is our secret,* Grandma had cautioned her, afraid of Mom's wrath. The Roths and their women always had secrets, no matter how banal.

There was a tunnel under the Spuyten Duyvil Speedway, now surely obliterated by a new, more efficient highway, perhaps the Henry Hudson? Not having a car to see for herself, Francine hadn't been up there in years.

Grandma would run down the steps and through the tunnel to the other side of the Speedway, leaving little Francine alone at the other end, and then, at a signal, she and Francine would run down their opposite steps into the tunnel to meet in the middle of the underground passage and greet each other with a hug! Later they would walk to a deli on Dyckman Street for crisp Kaiser rolls spread with sweet butter out of a huge wooden barrel.

Poor Mom! She had been so jealous of Grandma Roth and these imaginative outings with Francine. She claimed Grandma exposed Francine to unnecessary sexual risks. When Grandma said she had stripped Francine of her playsuit, because she had peed in it, and that a man passing by had stopped to look at the strapping little naked baby and comment on her beauty, Mom had screamed at Grandma. *How could you do such a thing!* Grandma protested. *But she's so beautiful!*

Poor Mom, later running crazily through the apartment brandishing a paring knife and threatening to kill Daddy if he didn't stop screwing "that dirty blonde" in 4G.

But not half as jealous as Francine when Percie made his ill-advised marriage to Nellie, the stuck-up Vassar graduate. Those were Percie's genuine crying days and Francine had become determined to rescue him from Nellie even if she had to murder her. Unfortunately Nellie had survived Percie's sudden death from a heart attack at age 67 by several months. Percie wasn't the one who was supposed to die first; Nellie was.

Even though Nellie was now dead, Francine still felt murderous when she remembered some of the scenes she had witnessed between Percie and Nellie, Nellie pounding him with her fists, screaming incoherently *I hate you, you big fat drunken bag of shit, I'll kill you, where's my gun,* looking around as though actually seeking the weapon, Percie cowering in the corner, his body shaking with supposed fear, whimpering, begging, pleading (in the same manner as he had when Christian used to pummel and bully him), Francine feeling murderous, not because Nellie might have been hurting Percie, oh no, this was Nellie playing the dominatrix, Nellie preparing Percie for sex…and Francine feeling murderous with jealousy. She had staked out a claim on Percie's body when they were twelve and now even after his death….well, an evil person like Nellie just couldn't be killed enough times!

Leafing through the *Bergdorf Goodman Magazine,* Francine was struck by a two-page spread of a Dior gown, similar to one that had come into the hotel shop the other day: black floral lace and ecru satin with a train, the whole fashioned from cotton, of all things. How odd! And it was selling for almost $10,000. It was so beautiful, Francine was wondering how she could smuggle it out of the shop. But where would she wear it?

Polly Hopkins, the shop manager, a skinny redhead with a sharp nose and the tongue to match, had definitely made herself one of Francine's targets by bawling her out that morning for 1) being late; 2) letting her "dirty" bra strap show at the neckline— *Don't you ever wash your underwear?…Not with rats in the basement where the washing machines are…What? Even in that fancy-schmancy building you live in? Anyway, there are many other ways of keeping things clean. I see that bra that you claim is grey, I see it every day. You don't change your bra frequently enough. Pretty soon the customers are going to complain about the way you smell*...and so on in this elevated vein.

Polly's third complaint for the day was that Francine had ignored a customer who was fingering the $4,850 scarlet ruched-bodice strapless gown in double-lace silk satin designed by couturier Angel Sanchez. This was another gown that Francine had her eye on. Except, once again, where would she ever wear it? Now if Percie were still alive, she would have made him take her down to New Orleans in it.... As for the "dirty" bra strap, Francine tried to explain to Polly that it was a grey satin bra, it wasn't "dirty"! Polly was near-sighted, not good for someone who professed to be a fashionista.

Are you listening, Francine? It was Polly again, butting in on Francine's plans for the Dior gown. *We could have sold that gown if you'd been paying attention...What? Listen Polly, you were so busy watching me ignoring the customer. Why didn't you go over there and help her yourself?...That's beside the point. I hired you to...blah, blah, blah....*

Then there were Polly's eternal orders. *Listen, go over there and straighten out those red satin cargo shorts, the ones with the bells on the pockets, no not those, not the long ones, the shorts, the shorts, why do I always have to repeat myself? You're not getting senile by any chance? And when you're finished with those....*

Now, in her cozy seat at the computer, Francine's dreams were allowed to swell and float on the rippling piano sounds of Art Tatum on her CD player, Tatum artfully fingering the arpeggios and fancy chords of *Yesterdays*, a very old song that was cruelly reminiscent of once dining with Percie in the late '50s in a midtown restaurant where an orchestra played *Yesterdays*, the old song not the Beatles' *Yesterday*, the present torture as she listened, gradually turning into clouds of pure memorial joy.

She would bring her big brown suede carryon into the shop some Friday and tell Polly she was taking the train right after work and going up to visit Bobo Jennings in Chatham for the weekend. The Dior would go into the empty bag and Francine would be on her way.

On further reflection, this didn't seem like such a clever plan after all. She would be an obvious suspect, especially if there weren't many customers that particular Friday, everyone going out to the Hamptons...Francine had no plans to go to prison for grand theft.

She and Percie used to pull off these stunts all the time, although on a much smaller scale. Long ago she and Percie had gone to Loew's State at Times Square to see a movie in which the heroine (Kim Novak?) had been wearing a silver chain necklace from which dangled a bold bright blue stone. Afterward, Percie the Instigator had urged her to steal a similarly garish necklace from Woolworth's. They had sidled up to the jewelry counter, marveling at how gaudy and cheap-looking the "jewels" were, waiting for the clerk to turn her back or go to another counter before Francine grabbed the necklace and dropped it into the roomy depths of her coat pocket. Percie said there was enough room in those deep pockets for the entire Woolworth's jewelry counter.

Outside the store, they had laughed themselves silly and then thrown the worthless bauble into the trash basket at the street corner.

At least now, she had another good story to channel to Percie through the good offices of the computer. *Are you sober, Percie? Is there any point in my trying to access you?*

Sometimes she felt like a huge ship, battering herself time after time against Percie as he lay listless, inert at the rim of the sandy shore, gradually floating out to sea, a dead whale, swollen with disease, hung over, staring sightlessly....

Belinda has made a copy of her employer's store key. This wasn't easy because her employer, Opal Mishman, has an eagle eye, or rather two eagle eyes of an unappetizing vapid grey, yet bright, searing, rapacious, the eagle eyes spread far apart on her rigid, sharp-chinned face looking somewhat like Nellie's in her fifties after she had lost 100 pounds at Weight Watchers.

Getting the key out of Opal's purse is not an easy job. To accomplish this, Belinda has to wait until there are no customers in the shop and Opal is in the lavatory doing god knows what, refastening her false eyelashes or mopping up her dripping mascara. Ah, finally, she has the key. It was buried in a side pocket of Opal's purse along with her credit cards and housekeys. Belinda had to wrench the store key off the fancy little sterling silver Tiffany key ring with the initials OM engraved on a small dangling sterling heart. Then she had to quickly secrete the key in the pocket of the skirt she had foresightedly worn that morning, the flowered rayon with the huge pocket in it that hid a piece of wax with which to make an imprint of the key. So that when Opal emerges finally from the lavatory, Belinda is to be seen studying the five-thousand dollar Cassin jacket in luna raine Scandinavian mink. Whatever "luna raine" is! Belinda wouldn't have stolen this piece of old lady shit for all the tea in China!

Then there is the matter of getting the key molded in the wax and back into Opal's purse. This is accomplished during Opal's next trip to the lavatory. Would Opal study the key and say What's the waxy stuff on the key? *Belinda decides, probably not.*

Now the long wait begins, first for the key copy at the locksmith's. Then for the break-in itself. You can imagine, Percie, that Belinda has to remain in the neighborhood of 63rd and Lex for a long time after she has ostensibly left work for the day. Why is Opal futzing around so long in the back of the shop? Is she getting herself off amidst the dingy back-of-behind crush of furs and furbelows? Oh, that was really impossible to imagine. Dried-up old bitch. Belinda retires to the nearest bar, unfortunately a walk of several blocks, and treats herself to a martini. With gin, please, and a twist.

At six o'clock Belinda walks back to the Cranberry [perhaps that name is too close to the real name "Cranbridge"], *always keeping in the forefront of her mind the dazzling image of the Dior gown—black floral lace, ecru satin—as inspiration for what she is about to do. The shop, facing on the deserted lobby, is dark. She has no trouble walking in, merely nodding at the concierge, explaining she has left her shopping bag in the store. She openly unlocks the door and walks in. She has indeed left the Bergdorf Goodman paper shopping bag in the back of the store and quickly stuffs the Dior into it. And marches out again, locking the door behind her, in full view now of a few hotel guests, the desk clerks and the concierge.*

Belinda boards the uptown train, almost empty at this hour after the commuter crush. Half an hour later she has reached the Central Park West station. She leaves the Bergdorf Goodman bag with its pricey cargo on the seat. She wonders who will find it....

That she was able to pull this off in full view of everyone gave Belinda a great sense of inner peace.

Francine leaned back in her chair and let her mind wander. The sounds of people treading softly down the carpeted hall beyond her door, their dim, unintelligible voices, the small but incisive click of an apartment door—all of it gave her a feeling of being of the world but not actually in it. The past where her mind wandered had become a vast plain of derring-do, groves of thin, dark cypress trees standing as sentinels for the knights-errant engaged in battle.

Aren't you proud of me, Percie?

As Francine remembered it, Percie's troubles with Nellie had started right off the bat, in fact, even before they were married. Francine had become determined to rescue Percie, her good friend, her childhood sweetheart, her beloved fool. Sober, he seemed to be asleep. Drunk, he came to life, doing an unconscious imitation of another falsely-admired cousin, the smarmy, voluble, hyperbolic history professor at Yale—Professor Nathaniel Roth, known to the children of the family as Cousin Natty-Bumppo, one of the rich Roths also in the snot-tasting tradition of Cousin Rollo with the added bonus of 65 years of deeply bitten-off fingernails so that Natty-Bumppo, heavy-handed and oblivious, grasped every hand stretched out to him in greeting with a hearty wrench, not because he was hearty but because he had lost all feeling at the tips of his fingers.

Percie would squirm in his chair, gesturing vaguely in every direction, his full, wet lips curling with the sterling political information he felt he was imparting, the very image of his cousin Natty. Was he consciously imitating him? Did he secretly admire him? Hard to say. *It has been said that the Soviet Union was the cradle of a series of cruel and relentless regimes. Not so. The Soviet Union did more for its people than any other nation in history, providing them with shelter, food, clothing, medical care, education, and all for free.* Professor Natty was one of the house radicals at Yale, the only one who espoused the Soviet cause. The others were Trotskyites and later, Maoists.

Like Rollo, Natty-Bumppo was a bulbous whale of a man, so obviously full of grievance and self-pity that he had been dubbed the Wounded Whale by his fellow alumni and even presented with a huge white Yale mug bearing the likeness of a blue whale and inscribed at the rim with "Wounded Whale".

Nellie, of course, could not tolerate Natty-Bumppo and his aggressively-stated politics so that Francine was often forced to side with her detestable cousin at infrequent family gatherings just out of a sense of family loyalty. Natty-Bumppo had gotten his Communist politics from his mother, a brilliant, beautiful card-carrying Jewish woman who would end each of her sentences on dialectical materialism with a sharp *Hunh?* And a glare at the victim she had verbally nailed to the wall. Lady Leah, as she was called privately and derisively by other Roths—and then later after the Bob Dylan song came out, *Lay Lady Leah*—had once run a manuscript service for Columbia students and faculty at the corner of 116th Street and Amsterdam Avenue. She claimed that during her heyday in the Village, she had one night slept between Eugene O'Neill and Djuna Barnes, and reported that both had been so drunk they only imagined they were being effective with her body. She was also the model for Henry Miller's *Rebecca Valentine* in *Sexus*. Some members of the Roth tribe had even spread the rumor that Natty-Bumppo was actually Miller's son, not a Roth at all.

All this being beside the point, family loyalty had forced Francine to side with Natty Bumppo against Nellie's conservatism.

"What do you know about being poor!" she had shouted at Percie's wife while Percie had murmured, snickering, in the background, "Nellie's idea of camping out is going from one luxury hotel to another."

And now... *What's this?* Francine had picked up a NYTimes on her way home and was leafing through the financial section to look at the day's quote for the blue-chip stock share she had recently sold to make a seriously overdue credit card payment. Selling her one share of stock—given to her by Percie—bothered her. The only comfort was the fact that the stock had not increased in value since she sold it. It was the only actual asset she had, its price having tripled from the original $1000 a buy-in share to almost $3000. *Shit! What's this?* A headline almost hidden at the bottom of the page swam up into her face. **Probe Opens in Stockbroker's Death.** Underneath was a small blurred photo of Percie taken at least twenty years before. She folded the paper abruptly.

She tried to remember the actual circumstances of Percie's death. He might have had some irritating characteristics but they were hardly bad enough to incite murder in anyone.

For instance, time meant nothing to Percie. If he and Francine were to rendezvous in a certain hotel room at 4 p.m., she might find him finally down in the hotel bar at 6 p.m. where he'd gotten stalled, eventually forgetting all about his date with her.

It had been different in the early days when Larry was a baby and Francine and Ray were still living in the city. Francine and Percie had sometimes enjoyed a few stolen moments together. Percie was more aggressive then. *I want to do this,* he had said, as they lay together on a hotel bed in midtown Manhattan. He squeezed her breasts together and sucked both nipples at once as though he were sucking for his life, as though he were actually drinking her milk, suckling her as though he had just come to the end of a long, dry crawl across the Sahara. Her nipples were sore for days afterward, a bittersweet reminder of Percie.

107

She had not been able to nurse Larry successfully. She had cried for days over this matter. *You're not a cow,* the doctor had said, laughing at her grief. Percie, or was it Christian, said her breasts were meant for sex, not motherhood. No help for a nursing mother in those days.

Sometimes she and Percie got very drunk together, taking turns sucking solace from the gin bottle and each other. At such times, they cried boisterously in each other's arms, matching their sobs in a frenzy of melodrama, and never actually getting around to having full-blown sex.

Another time, another hotel room. It's a quiet place, the walls done up in drab colors of beige and mauve. When Francine looks out the window she sees the moon is a big, round, white-hot disc in the eastern sky. She looks down from their 10th floor window to the dark objects below, people moving ever so slowly along the pavement, like somnolent, dying roaches. She expects to see them turning over on their backs, legs wiggling helplessly in the air.

They don't get drunk this time. They have wild sex, Francine pinning Percie to the bed by his arms, lying between his widespread legs, his huge herniated belly rising high above his genitals, she lying between his legs while she ravages his body with her lips and tongue and teeth, the big moon watching them through the window. Francine is on fire waiting for Percie to penetrate her. It doesn't happen for hours and hours. Then they fall asleep for a long time on opposite sides of the bed. They sleep like babies.

Francine pondered the meaning of Percie's huge belly. When a surgeon had finally had to remove Percie's gall bladder and then a few months later his colon, the doctor had said Percie's organs were huge, the largest he'd ever seen. Was this part of Percie's trouble, his body trying to encompass these massive organs? Was this the cause of his sluggishness? And ultimately his alcoholism?

Oh, no use trying to figure out the why of alcoholism for Percie or for anyone else on earth.

She preferred to think about Percie regaling her with stories of his sexual exploits—how he had left this one at the altar, how he had cheated on that one the day their engagement was announced. How he had spent his wedding night with a hooker, explaining to Nellie he was going to a poker game instead, that he had a "prostate problem" and couldn't get it up for her anyway. He enjoyed describing Nellie's screams of rage as he fled down the stairs from their swank honeymoon rooms at the Plaza and out to the freedom of the brothel in Tudor City.

After awhile, growing into middle age and weighing close to 300 pounds, Percie would claim having sex with Francine was too hard on his heart. But even with this deprivation, the memory of his breath, tainted with whiskey, cigars and salami po-boys slathered with garlic-embedded horse radish—a bold combination that bolstered the famous Roth males' "hot tongue"—could still give Francine a thrill. Then, of course, over the years, the concept of "hot tongue" had suffered downward slippage so that more recently it referred to the penis.

Who would want to kill Percie?

Chapter Three

The blue light was twinkling again. Francine thought Percie had died of a heart attack and here was a *Times* item stating that the police were hinting Percie had been murdered!

Christian should know about this. He had married a crazy named Castillie, who pretended to be a former actress. She was one of Percie's favorite targets. *Did you notice how bowed her legs are in those short tight skirts? She looks worse than Nellie.*

Sometimes Francine wondered if Percie talked about her to others the way he talked about Nellie and Castillie.

Christian and Castillie had three grown children (and some grandchildren that Francine had lost track of) and were now living at the far eastern end of Long Island. Christian had just closed out a very successful career as a corporation lawyer. His phone number was somewhere—where—where? Francine ransacked the jumble of notes and bills and charge card statements that filled the computer table drawers. Where was her address book, her bible, her main connection to the outside world? Containing email codes, phone numbers, doctors' addresses, appointments never kept....

She made a date to meet Christian at O'Clanahan's on Seventh Avenue, said to have once been a Belfast communication point. Certainly there was enough Irish brogue in the place—a regular Babel of lilting tongues. And they served the best fried onion rings and BLTs in Christendom. And there was Christian, carrying on the tradition of the sturdier members of the Roth brotherhood, nursing a Scotch as though of no importance to him, which it probably wasn't, and discussing in his flatly precise voice, so different from Percie's warm, plangent voice— discussing the Yankees' prospects with the eager barmaid. *What do you think of this new first baseman?...*The bar was crowded, tables jammed, noise level at its maximum. *I said...I heard you...Where's that retarded teenager I saw you with at Percie's funeral?...I beg your pardon.* Christian gave her his intense, angry stare. Smooth and sleek. Narrow, blazing brown eyes, olive skin, still a full head of slightly curling salt and pepper hair. He could have been Algerian. Francine had seen many men of his physical type in her single visit to Strasbourg and wondered if the Roths had originally migrated from Africa....

How's Castillie? Christian's wife, a massive redhead, hair worn in a fluffy cloud to conceal the slight balding. She was thin-lipped and angry, her soft, mean voice so disembodied you had to strain to hear her. She was clearly insane. Her gibberish made little sense: *There are three main ways of communication...* Christian took pleasure in baiting his wife of 40 years. *And what would that be, Castillie, dear?...Consider this: The three ways are reading, writing, and rehearsing.* Castillie had been on the stage briefly, or so she claimed, in Baltimore. Baltimore, of all places!

And Loup, how's Loup? Francine asked, referring to Christian's oldest son, a longtime alcoholic. She had to shout over the noise of the bar. She remembered that Christian had once blamed Percie, unreasonably, for Loup's drinking. *Since Percie had no kids, he let his seed go through me to Loup.* Christian shrugged. He didn't want to talk much about Loup. *He's fine. He's into photography now...Oh really? Pornography?...Hell, no! Open your ears. I said photography... With what goal in mind?* But it was no good needling Christian. He had a rhino hide and wouldn't have recognized an insult if it were laid on his dinner plate.

Here's the thing, Francine. I've talked to the D.A.

Yes, certainly Christian would have talked to the D.A. Francine pictured him sitting across a massive desk from some self-important City Hall D.A., Christian so slick and hard, a dead person only pretending to be alive.

The thing is, Francine, I've talked to the D.A. and the nurse claims she was gone for fifteen minutes and when she returned to his room, all his tubes were unplugged. He still had a pulse but he didn't respond when she asked him how he was feeling. She plugged him in again. Next thing she knew—she says you were there the whole time—you must know more about his death than anyone, no?...You're not going to pin this on me, Christian. As far as I know, he was plugged in the whole time. Maybe the nurse killed him. Who are you going to believe? Maybe Percie had promised to leave her a lot of money...He'd probably forgotten he didn't have any. Christian had given up on Percie a long time ago. *Yes, his brain was ruined. Memory totally false. He was on the verge of wet brains...What's that?...Brains turned to mush. Probably if you could have looked inside Percie's skull you'd have seen a lot of milky mush. Last time I saw Percie, maybe a year ago, He claimed he'd taken you to Paris and bought you a big diamond...What!...Yeah, a diamond as big as the Ritz, that's how he phrased it. Do you have a diamond that big?...I don't have any diamonds! I mean I was in Paris once but with some other guy, not Percie.*

Sipping her martini, Francine felt very sad. *Percie was always like that, Christian. He would say anything to please anyone…Yeah, he would tell Mother he had brushed his teeth and she knew he was lying, but what could she do? You're still carrying it for him, aren't you, Francine? Even though you know that alcohol had turned him into the worst liar!...Everyone lies, Christian. People lie all the time. They can't live without their lies. None of us can.* Francine paused. Here was something Christian probably didn't know…that she had left Ray and her son Larry and California altogether in hopes of getting Percie away from Nellie, of being with Percie, a Percie already impotent from drink. She decided not to tell Christian. What was the use? Percie was dead.

O'Clanahan's had become noisier. A stocky Irishman named Kevin had brought out his guitar and was playing and singing militant Irish ballads. *We're not Irish, Francine. Can we go to a quieter place?...I like this place. Percie liked it. He said he was in here one night when someone, some IRA enthusiast, pulled a gun on someone else he claimed was a "bloody Brit"…*

Oh, that's such bullshit. You didn't believe that, did you?...But that kind of stuff was happening then in the early '80s. There was a lot going on in Northern Ireland. A lot of so-called traitors were coming over here and the militants were after them…Bullshit…No, I mean it, Christian…How come you know so much about the Irish stuff?...I was there, in San Francisco in the early '80s. Ray and I used to hang out at the Plough and the Stars. It was a great Irish bar. Lots of intrigue. Didn't we bring you there once when you and Castillie came out to the Coast? Revolution was rampant. Percie was right. People had guns. It was Belfast transplanted to the States, raising money for the revolution, and what better place than San Francisco where anything goes?...

How do you know what Percie said was truth or fiction? Don't you see, alcohol gave Percie license to do and say anything he damn well pleased? He was always self-delusional. He would have made a great soldier; he would never have believed he was going to get killed except in his fantasies. He lied to himself most of all. Percie, the great martyr. Percie just feeling oh! so sorry for himself. Percie had his little racket going, his way of saying fuck you *to the world. It was too much of an image he prided himself on—being a roaring, raving*

112

drunk. Even if he had stopped drinking, he would never have admitted it. It worked too well for him. What a liar!...Even so, Christian, you know he had to lie to himself and everyone else because you persecuted him when he was young. I remember so well how you guys were always wrestling on the living room floor, Percie always getting the worst of it from you, crying and yelling when you kept hurting him...And he was twice as strong as I was, Francine. You could see that, couldn't you? He enjoyed the martyrdom of giving in to me. Always the aggrieved one.

Anyway, that wasn't it, Francine. It was Mother. She put all the pressure on me because I was older. I had to pass it on to Percie. Actually, I protected him. Anyway, why are we arguing the point? You and I survived the Roths. Percie didn.t' Listen, Francine, Percie was the most frightened person I knew. Even as a kid if he fell down and got a scrape and got bloody, he would run into the house screaming with terror, claiming he'd broken his leg!

But I had the greatest respect for Percie on the ball field. He almost made it to the Majors, with our dad guiding his career. Our dad played semi-pro baseball one summer up in Canada, did you know that?

Francine said she remembered something about Uncle Henry's interest in sports. *I guess I was already in California with Ray when all this was going on. The fact is, Percie once told me he envied me my "durability". I never though much about his muscles and what he could do with them, except in bed...Well, that was the heart of him, Francine darling...*Christian lifted her hand and kissed the back of it—*his dreaming athletic heart that he almost fulfilled. The drinking was a big racket to punish everyone for his own failures...Or was it a matter of finding love in a bottle, Christian?...Some people just can't get enough love, Francine.*

The martinis were accomplishing their task; Francine found she had to suppress giggles. *Maybe Percie was murdered by an IRA assassin. Remember how he always said he'd like to go off to South America and fight with some of the Red Brigade, Percie called them the Red Flame—anyway, whatever they were called—those so-called Peruvian liberators or at least I think they were Peruvian...What are you babbling about? Peruvian assassins killed Percie? In his hospital bed?...Not the Peruvians, the IRA. Don't you think that's a funny idea?*

Christian didn't seem to think her fantasy was particularly amusing. He resumed his conversation about the Yankees with the barmaid who was now leaning on the bar, her Millie the Milkmaid breasts pushing against her low-cut peasant bodice.

Francine nudged him. *Oh by the way, Christian, are you listening? I have some wonderful poetry at home that Percie wrote while hw was drunk. It was about eight years ago. He sent me a sheaf of wonderful poems, so rueful, so right on. They're a little like Bukowski, only better, I think. Of course, I'm prejudiced…Who the hell is Bukowski?…Oh, a dead poet. Dead now. Very alcoholic while alive. Don't worry about it. Don't you want to read some of Percie's stuff? I could email a couple of poems to you. There's one he called* Crazy *that I've memorized. I think it's really funny. It goes like this:*

The barmaid had been listening to their conversation. Now she shouted to the crowd. *Listen, everyone, this lady here wants to recite a poem.* She had Francine turn around on her stool and face the jammed tables. The barmaid turned down the TV sound and Francine cleared her throat while Christian hunkered down on his stool, afraid of what he was going to hear. The blue light flickered and flashed frantically before Francine's eyes as she spoke:

This is called "Crazy"—I wish the crazy lady next door/ would do some ranting:/ I need reassurance.

The barmaid shook her head. *Is that it? I thought it was going to be about troubles.*

Francine felt dizzy. She reached over and kissed Christian goodbye on the cheek as someone shouted *Don't we all need reassurance? Never enough reassurance!* Francine slipped off the stool and headed for the door as people clapped desultorily behind her. Christian was shouting behind her: *Please don't email me any poems, Francine. They're too Percie for me.*

She turned and waved again to Christian. Poor old thing. He had to go home to Castillie. He always had to go home to her, no matter how many teenagers or barmaids he screwed, nor in how many Manhattan hotel rooms. Or did he take them to his Yale club now? Or to the New York Athletic Club? Did he still have a membership there? In his youth he had talked about his encounters with famous male movie stars—many of them gay—Edward Everett, Brian D, and others. He'd been starstruck, but no longer. Christian had had his fill of celebrities. He was almost one himself, having been involved in a probe of insider trading. Being an extremely clever man, he'd come out clean as a whistle.She rode the subway up to 72nd Street where the station was so brutally hot it took her breath away as she stepped from the train onto the narrow platform. Christian's words tossed and turned in her brain. *I talked to the D.A.* So he had wasted no time in consulting authorities. He probably knew most of them by their first names. She shivered in a spasm of fear. So Percie had told Christian he had bought her a diamond in Paris.

Percie…Drink had really started to destroy his brain. She had heard of one of his escapades in London. A mutual friend had written to her to say that Percie had arrived at hr house in Portman Place straight from Heathrow and he was "drunk, dirty and without money". Then another friend had put him up for a week in a hotel where Percie became so unruly with drink, the manager had to call the police. Percie was then taken to a hospital with severe drs where he spent a week before being released.

Francine then began getting feverish communiqués…he had no money, but he had learned to panhandle for drinks, he told her proudly. Later he wrote pitiful letters saying he had developed bronchitis, then pneumonia, had lost 50 pounds, needed a gall bladder operation. At that point, Christian had stepped in and guaranteed the American consulate in London Percie's airfarr if they would just put him on a plane to JFK.

Confronted with all this by Francine, Percie had denied it: *It wasn't like that at all. I arrived with plenty of money and wined and dined all my old pals for a week. Jail? No way.* Memory totally pickled in alcohol.

At home now Francine stripped down and turned out the lights—even light bulbs generated unwanted heat—and turned on the A/C full blast before lying down on the futon. She was trying to remember her last visit to Percie at St. Vincent's. Had he jokingly said, *Pull the plug* or had she

said it? Had there been previous 'pull the plug'
conversations? The only thing she remembered of that final
day beside Percie's hospital bed was that she had a secret
for him. She couldn't even remember now what the secret
was. She had a lot of secrets. Her memory was going.
Perhaps she was near death. Maybe she would soon be
joining Percie. She wanted to join him wherever he was.

It was like a dream—was she really awake?—as she
recapitulated her long, long affair with Percie. There was so
much pain in it.

There was Percie in bed on the sleeping porch in
Greenwich. But then Christian had been with them,
horning in, so to speak. Even earlier as children, she and
Percie had sat in the languid waters near the shore of the
Sound, their bottoms submerged, and stroked each other
through their bathing suits. There were their teenage years
when they slyly eluded Christian and made love on the
beach at midnight, sometimes swimming that brief way
across the Sound to Belle Haven when there were lots of
huge old trees to hide their fun. Then later the Manhattan
hotel rooms…

And then for awhile, it seemed now like just a few
minutes, this all came to a halt when Percie told her that
one miserable cold day in January at the Ship Ahoy on
Madison Avenue where they warmed themselves with
B&Bs that he had decided to marry Nellie. All that
Francine could remember of this conversation was Percie's
idiotic words as she stared unbelievingly into ships' fittings,
garlands of net, bone-white life rings with ships' names on
them, lifeboats cut in half to fit the décor and Francine
frantically thinking *That's what I need—a lifeboat or at least a
lifejacket.*

Not that Nellie hadn't been in the picture before.
Someone in Francine's city crowd once brought Nellie up to
Greenwich to flesh out a party of four couples. Was it
Christian? Francine couldn't remember. All she
remembered was that Percie had devoted all his attention to
Nellie, Nellie at that time so long and stringy and athletic.
And very rich, her father a Park Avenue doctor with cases
of Mumms in his hall closet. Francine remembered that the

three couples of them had piled into someone's jalopy and driven into the city at midnight to steal a case while Nellie's parents were gone for the weekend, then brought it up to Greenwich where they got wonderfully drunk. How could Percie be so crass as to marry this rich girl with champagne in the closets! On the other hand, how could he resist?

But then later, after the elaborate wedding out on the penthouse terrace, forty-five floors above Park Avenue, Percie had called Francine. *Hey, kiddo, let's have some fun. This married life is too much for me!,,,What? You mean living in Daddy's penthouse on Park Avenue isn't good enough for you? I could have told you that. Didn't I warn you about getting married? Especially to that bitch?* But Francine was happy to give in to Percie. They began meeting on a regular basis. Until she met and married Ray—she had to get married sometime, didn't she? And she wanted a baby—some substitute for her blind love for Percie. Eventually they moved West. Where she had stayed for 40 years—with occasional trips to the East—waiting for Nellie to die or for Percie to divorce her.

And now, at three o'clock in the morning in real time, there was a disturbance outside her door. It was Bob, Bob only 35 but already with the gaunt, leathery face of a cadaver, and now—as she opened her door a crack and peeked out into the hall—he actually was a cadaver. Medics were carrying his long bones out on a gurney, pushing their way through a crowd of whispering tenants, Bob's emaciated body concealed under a blanket. Even his face. That meant he was dead, no?

How did he die?...Hanging, I think...Who found him?...His girlfriend. At least I think that's what happened. Where is she, anyway?...His girlfriend? She certainly left in a hurry...I think the cops took her away for questioning. Something about a bloody brick...Well, you can't hang yourself with a bloody brick. What was he trying to do in there? Build a fireplace?

Much guffawing. People were starting to get hilarious with a touch of hysteria thrown in, making jokes about Bob's body. Gradually, as the body disappeared into the freight elevator and was on its way down to the street, people dispersed or stood in knots discussing the so-called tragedy. Francine shivered and retreated back to her nest. No more loud music in the early hours, that was for sure. Well, she had wanted him dead for disturbing her sleep night after night and now he was dead. She must have some secret powers! She was trying to remember the exact nature of her encounters with Bob. God, her memory was getting terrible. Whatever these encounters had been, they would make a good story for Percie.

Francine closed the door and went back to sleep. She dreamed she was Liane dePougy, the famously beautiful French courtesan of the Belle Epoque. She was lying atop Liane's pale blue satiny bedsheets, planning a surprise for the eager suitor knocking at her door. Then Bob entered the room and raced toward her outstretched body, her arms and legs finally wide apart after refusing him a dozen times, Bob inexplicably a French count who was hot for her and wanted to give her diamonds, and Bob slipping out of his clothes, couldn't wait to get to her, panting and foaming, penis rising to undreamed of heights, rising perpendicular to the rest of his emaciated body, throwing himself on the outsized circular bed and then on hands and knees going between her legs, almost there, breathless, licking her fur, and then, and then, letting out a stupendous *fart* that surely could be heard as far as the doorman outside, or at least to the reception desk downstairs, or at least out to the elevator. Francine/Liane first giggling and then screaming at him in a rage. *Get out! Get out! You disgusting gasbag! Canaille! Fucking jerk! Get out of my room! Leave me alone! And take your stupid farts with you!*

When she awoke early next morning she could hardly wait to transmit her dream to Percie. He would think it was really funny, funnier than her story about being in bed with a famous lesbian who was hopelessly drunk and who was doing strange things to Francine's nipples while a seven year old neighbor child looked on, a frightened look on her face. Francine had felt sorry for the little girl—how lonely she must have been to have suddenly appeared at the side of their bed—while Ray and the child's mother sat in chairs next to the bed animatedly talking to each other, ignoring Francine and the famous lesbian (Djuna?

Nathalie?). Francine felt so sorry for the little girl, she invited her into bed to make a cozy threesome....

No, this dream about Bob was even funnier than anything that had ever happened to Francine/Liane.

I'm starting to dream things on my own, Percie. I don't need a book to provide me with material.

Hey, I wish you would get in touch with me...somehow...please? It would make me so happy.

Knocking at her door. Well, that was to be expected, wasn't it? It was the cops trying to get information. *Did you hear anything unusual, Miss?* Francine preferred to be called "Madame" or better yet, "Mademoiselle". Laugh out loud or l.o.l., the cipher-initials if you happened to be in an online chat room. People were so illiterate now they were starting to speak in acronyms. It was bound to happen.

However, Francine kept the laugh to herself as she invited the cops into her studio. She knew it was only prudent to treat the cops seriously. They looked all grumpy and self-righteous, probably the way Great Grandpa Zimmer looked as he lorded it over his so-called Raines Law hotel with prostitutes running in and out at all hours of the day and night, dirty brawling city streets, constant battle against rats, Grandma hidden away behind the skirts of her own grandmother. Parrot squawking in her ears, shutting out the world beyond. No way to know what it was really like. No way to dip into the past and find out. Did they ever allow Grandma outside the house? Perhaps only for grammar school, dancing lessons, piano lessons. She and her brothers had been given the works at the expense of hookers. *This is our secret.* Had Grandma actually ever said that?

Officers, I didn't hear a damn thing. It was as quiet as the grave around here until the neighbors started making a hubbub...One of them told us you objected to the deceased's loud music, is that true?...Well, I may have complained about it a couple of times, but actually—well, I hate to say this, but we were very close, very intimate you might say...Oh?...Yes, Bob and I were going to get married...

It was hard to suppress giggles, remembering her Liane dePougy dream, as she imparted this information because if there was one thing Francine enjoyed doing it was stringing the cops along. Even at her own risk. Percie had called her a risk-taker, which Percie himself certainly never was. Or if so, he had to be drunk. Percie, Percie. She couldn't wait for the cops to leave so that she could get back on the computer before she had to go to work.

Oh, and she must call Bobo. If she were in trouble about Bob, she would need Bobo to hide her up in Chatham. Deserted countryside, trees, hills, rutted dirt roads, lovely white frame house, bedrooms sequestered under the upstairs eaves, cool pond to dip into, an adorable apricot poodle named Maggie to play with, a martini in hand, a very dry martini, icy with Stoly straight from the freezer. *I slipped into the nearest martini and disappeared for weeks!*

The cops were now poking around the studio, looking everywhere.

You don't seem very upset about your fiancé's death. Say, what are all these bricks doing back here?...Trying to stop up the mouseholes...Mind if we take one? They were making leave-taking noises. *Oh, by the way, stay in town. We may need to talk to you again...Yessir...* The cops were mumbling to each other as they left. *She's full of herself...She's full of shit...*

Francine closed the door on them and shuddered. Another grinding day at the Cranbridge shop to look forward to under Polly's near-sighted, peering eyes. Polly was too vain to wear glasses. Francine thought maybe she would try swiping something from the store right under Polly's nose. It would be a real challenge, one that Percie would appreciate. And maybe another visit from the cops.

Must get in touch with Bobo. Now where was his number? And she hadn't paid the phone bill yet. A wonder the phone company would let her call long distance, or maybe that wasn't how it worked in the billing department.

She kept messing around in the drawer until she found the Chatham number

Marjorie answered. God, what a smug, self-righteous voice she had. She should have been a cop. But not to self-righteous this time. *Francine, I'm so glad you called. I guess you've heard, or read in the* Times?...*What are you talking about?*

It seemed that everyone was dying, even Bobo. Francine remembered, irrelevantly, how surprised she'd been when she had read recently the obituary of a former high school classmate at George Washington High who had become a police chief in a New Jersey town, a boy she'd always respected for his sincerity, Frank...Couldn't remember his last name. Some Irish name. She should have married some calm, judicious man like Frank, not an excitable loud-mouth like Ray, a man you couldn't sleep with, who snored at night, whose toenails were an inch long—wounding weapons, they were. She'd moved out of his bed. Had moved into it and married him in the first place because, because she couldn't have Percie, because Ray was there, wanting her badly, and asked her to...Marjorie was answering. *Hello? Hello?* Marjorie sounded uncharacteristically frantic.

Bobo died night before last—peaceful—in his sleep—heart failure...Shall I come up, oh yes, I'll come up, like a death in the family, my boss will understand [like hell she will!]...Oh no, no need for that—memorial service next month at the church here in Chatham—everyone's being so nice—gotta go now, Marjorie's voice catching finally as the finality of Bobo's death struck her, talking about it to Francine, Bobo's oldest friend, part of the old Roth family...so close to the Jennings...*oh dear*...ending in a sob...

All Francine's helpers were drying, for what were friends and lovers but "helpers", helping you get through the day somehow or other. Only in her failing brain were their stories being kept alive. They mustn't be forgotten. Bobo's story—his father a speakeasy bartender who beat up Bobo's mother Kate and made dates with other women on the phone right in front of Kate, beating Kate until year-old little Bobo standing watching from his crib got so upset he vomited. Bobo being raised by his Irish grandmother, living in the apartment on West 125th where 14-year-old Bobo teased Francine with his cat. *It's gonna get you! It hates you!...I'm not afraid.*

Ranting and raving about "the Jews" all around them. You lived in your neighborhood and took on its prejudices, the need to look down on others. Kate killed in

121

a crash on her way home from work in Yonkers. It was three o'clock in the morning. Why was Kate coming home so late? Was she sleeping with her boss? She'd said no to marriage. She'd said, "once bitten, twice shy". Speeding home, drunk maybe, crashing into the big truck parked by the side of the road, no lights to warn her, Kate's chest crushed in against the wheel. Bobo and Nana moving up to the more sedate, middle-class streets of Kingsbridge to live with his aunt and uncle.

Everyone dying, Percie. I might as well be dead, too. Speak to me, Percie...Christ, I hope I don't have to give up this apartment!

Chapter Four

Christl! So hot!

It was Saturday and Francine Roth was carrying a water bottle as she inched her way down Columbus Avenue toward the movie theater. It was 104 degrees, too insanely hot to leave her cool studio. She looked downward to see her usually slender ankles dangerously pink and swelling. The left one was the worst. It actually puffed out over the strap of her sandal. Time for the blue light to twinkle?

She had hoped to treat herself to lunch at a favored restaurant near her apartment but their A/C had broken down and they had had to close, the servers standing around disconsolately in wilting whites, the front door open, more readily to throw the city's long dark creeping shadows onto the tiled floors. Francine was disappointed. They served the best gravy and mashed potatoes, even better than the Schatsi in Santa Monica.

Well, it was too hot to eat.

She finally made it into the theater at 66th Street where a crowd was milling around, trying to decide which movie to attend. She felt she could stand to see almost any one of the six or eight movies offered, but finally settled on "The Man Who Wasn't There". She thought Billy Bob was repulsive, so thin, so dry. She'd heard that after making this particular movie he'd gone into the hospital with anorexia and indeed he walked stiffly through the movie as though his joints were hurting. But the movie was a piece of genius, on a par with "The Usual Suspects". Francine saw one carefully-selected movie a month.

And halfway through the complicated plot (one character actually said the story behind the killing was giving him a headache), she realized Percie was trying to get a message across to her. He was taking the form of the character played by James Gandolfini, one of Francine's favorites from "The Sopranos", big, fat guy, big barrel of a belly, old belly barrel, another belly like Percie's where a woman could lay her head to rest in solid comfort.

As Gandolfini sat behind his large desk, supposedly confronting Billy Bob, he spoke to Francine: *I know all about*

Nellie and what you did to her. Francine squirmed in her seat. *And I forgive you. I hated her anyway. Old bitch! But Jesus, get those bricks out of your apartment. And that's the best I can do for you. See you in Heaven, Francine.*

So Francine was quite disappointed when Gandolfini's character was killed during the scene. It was that stupid autistic Billy Bob.

Coming out of the theater into brilliant sunshine and heat, Francine wondered how long the city would continue to stand now that the new millenium had begun and now that the Trade Towers had been so rudely, and worse, so easily, toppled. She walked slowly up Columbus, wishing she could go into the restaurant at the Beaux Arts and have a very expensive, very luscious dinner. Sipping at her water bottle, she tried to keep to the shade of storefronts. Some even had awnings.

She remembered a short story she had read as a kid, out of Mom's *Saturday Evening Post*, a science fiction story about cavemen a few centuries hence who crawled along the New Jersey meadows to the shores of a river where a sign poked up out of the mud, a sign that read "udson River". And beyond the river, according to the pale black and white illustration that headed the story, were the towering ruins of the city. And the cavemen stared at them in awe. They wondered what place it was, or what it had been. And that would be the human condition of some year like 3064.

She wished for Percie's lips on hers, his hands gently trailing along her skin. She wished to hear him play the piano again, doing his deep, throaty Al Jolson imitation of "You Made Me Love You".

Which she now saw as a joke because who or what did Percie ever love except the bottle?

At home again and a message from Marjorie was playing as Francine entered the studio. *I'm very sorry, my dear, I'm going to have to sell the studio you've been renting from us. Now that Bobo is gone….*

Francine stood quietly by the machine as Marjorie's voice faded and disappeared, back through the phone wires that had spawned her fatal words.

Francine would have to look to Christian for help.

In her lifelong pursuit of Percie that every once in awhile she began to see as useless, even silly, she had neglected the other important things in her life like her husband during the long years she was married to him, her son Larry, money....She must call Larry....

I know the map of your body by heart. That's what Percie had once told her.

Well, okay, Christian was saying now as Francine begged him to help her. *I'm about to be evicted...Okay,* he said, *if you want to come out here to Montauk and help me with Castillie. She's getting worse by the day. You should have seen her last night....*

Be the caretaker for a madwoman? Francine remembered the last time she had visited them in Montauk. Their rambling white frame bungalow sat on a wild road that led ultimately to the end of the Point and its famous lighthouse. There was a mailbox on the road with four simple letters—ROTH. It had reminded Francine of Cape May, its own wild coast, rushes poking up out the sand, the old lighthouse, tourists' boat going out into the ocean for sightings of dolphins, the studied quaintness of the town's old houses whose interiors were now a sight for moneyed tourists. Pretentiously charming....

The weekend several years ago when Francine had stayed in the Montauk house, Castillie had been carrying a rag doll around the house, speaking in its supposed high-pitched soft little voice, then the singsong screech, *I'm a little dolly and I love to sing. Que sera, sera, how much is that doggy in the window?...*How could Christian stand it? Francine and Christian had gotten very drunk on his wonderfully icy Stoly martinis while Castillie continued singing, fluff of red hair atop a balding dome, wandering from room to room, animating the doll with her terrible madness. *What's the matter, Christian, no Zoloft for this poor lunatic?...I don't believe in all these modern medications. It's all poison...Sooner or later, Christian, we all have to die, poison or no poison...I prefer to live as long as possible, thank you very much, Francine.*

They had snuggled up in her guestroom bed that night, hours after Castillie had fallen into her own bed on the other side of the house. *No pills?* Francine had thought. *Christian must be totally deluded.*

The woman was monumentally out of it on prescription drugs that made her want to lie in bed all day, or waltz around the house with her toys to the tune of her very own crack-brained music. The medicine chest in the master bathroom—peered into by Francine on one of her prowls around the house while Castillie and Christian were out running errands—was filled to capacity with valium, atavan, Nembutal, darvocet, percodan, and even some pills from earlier times like librium, even milltown. The woman wasn't insane, she was a drug addict. Was this, too, a random, but inevitable condition of being part of the Roth family?

Francine and Christian had snuggled up and watched Clint Eastwood movies on the dvd player until five in the morning. *It's Sunday. We can sleep all day...I'm thinking of putting Castillie in a nursing home...That would be a good solution.*

An idea Christian had apparently abandoned since he was now asking Francine to come and take care of Castillie. Sometimes Francine was touched by Castillie's antics, understanding that contrary to all appearances, the woman was trying hard to achieve sanity in an insane world. Still, a brick to the back of her head would put everyone around her out of their misery. Francine thought she might pack a brick in her carryon. You never knew when it would come in handy.

And Christian. He had seemed hostile after Percie's death. At their recent meeting at O'Clanahan's, Christian had seemed devoid of all mutual memory or feeling, except for that random kiss of her hand. He had seemed to hold her responsible for Percie's death. Now that the probe into Percie's death had been dropped for insufficient evidence....Francine had read about it that very morning in the *Times* and heaved a big sigh of relief. Now Christian would be friendlier.

Marjorie hadn't heard from Francine so her messages were getting more hostile. *You have to leave as soon as possible, Francine. Please get in touch with me. I need to find a buyer for that place right away. Then the tenants' association has to approve. It's all so tiresome.*

126

Things were getting edgy. *Rough edges drear…was that* Dover Beach, *the Matthew Arnold poem?* She had memorized a lot of poetry at Hunter. It was the thing to do in those days. You memorized *J Alfred Prufrock*—T.S. Eliot by the yard. *A pair of ragged claws scuttling across the ocean floor….*

Percie was just a sodden lump of alcoholic shit. That's what Christian had called him. Francine had to agree. *A sodden lump. Percie, you sodden lump, I'm in trouble here. And you're not here to help me out. Not that he ever had. Been. Able. To.*

Bags packed, down in the elevator, past the Hispanic concierge—*hasta la vista*—smiles all around—and into Christian's jazzed-up Honda convertible idling at the curb, the top down, the seats seeming to be sitting on the road. Francine fell into the car, helped gallantly by Philip the doorman. Philip making a joke as he hoisted her carryon into the trunk. *What have you got in here, madame, a body?…Don't be silly, Philip…*

The motor was already running. Christian was wearing goggles and one of Castillie's brightly-colored scarves around his neck…*Who do you think YOU are? Isadora Duncan?…Ha ha! Just trying to keep the back of my neck warm in the breeze. Like to keep the top down when the weather is as nice as it is today.*…She had always feared the back of Christian's neck, something so stalwart and male about it. Percie had no neck, his large head squatting directly on his meaty shoulders.

Now the Beatles were soberly present on the CD player…*When I'm sixty-four—Will you still need me, will you still feed me…*Francine had passed the age of 64 several years ago, she thought idly, looking out over dingy and ever-so-old and tiresomely familiar streets and bridges on the way out to the Island. You could take the girl out of the city, but you couldn't take the city out of the girl.

Well, she was sure glad to stiff Polly Hopkins and the Cranbridge dress shop. *You're leaving me in the lurch,* Polly had panted when Francine quit over the phone. *Thought you'd be glad to be rid of me…What are you saying, darling? I'm crazy about you. Just because you wouldn't go to bed with me…*Had Polly actually said that or was it Francine's blue sparkle playing tricks on her again? So many women nowadays claimed they lost opportunities because they refused to sleep with their lady-bosses. Sexism in double-reverse.

Long Island flying by, didn't Jackson Pollock used to live around here someplace? Once did, now dead. Signs pointed here, there and everywhere—East Hampton where Grandpa Roth had driven a meat delivery wagon around to the houses of rich people during the summer of 1914, the closest thing he had done with meat since 1906 when he had gambled away his two inherited butcher shops, one in Yorkville and the other in the Bronx. Daddy and Henry had gone out there to spend the summer with him, happily riding the meat wagon over the dusty roads from one huge pile of a beach cottage to another. Daddy had so hoped, he once told Francine, that his parents would get together again but it never happened. So back to the Sheltering Arms went Daddy and Uncle Henry.

Now Grandpa lay in Green-wood Cemetery, a deliberate suicide or an asphyxiation by the accident of turning on the illuminating gas lamp without lighting it. He had come in drunk, no doubt, into his Bronx roominghouse. Francine pictured a dark crummy room with torn shades, gas-hissing lamp in the wall, rusty iron bedstead. 1923. So be it. Goodbye, Grandpa. Over and over again, her family history. What was the use of it? Possibly because she was about to join her ancestors? Her supposed loved ones? Up there in Roth heaven someplace?

She imagined them dwelling in a big cloud high above the city, pointing things out to each other. *I remember when they built the first subway in 19 ought 2…Oh look! They've torn down the Hippodrome! Penn Station! The Winter Garden! It ain't what it used to be.* And Francine thought, *there never were and there never would be any "good old days".* Back to the ancestors. *Hey, whadja think about the Trade Towers going down?…Think? I think they didn't build them right. The Empire State would have weathered ten jet-fuelled missiles. Remember when a plane crashed into it in the '40s?…Remember? How could I forget? Mae Shea was there, walking along 34th street, when it happened. She said when the plane hit, she went straight into the nearest bar…Remember Mae, that crazy drunken broad that used to fall out of bed all the time? Bobo's Nana practically raised her. Mae's* *mother was a lush, too...* Francine thought her loved ones were probably pausing to dish Mae for awhile. Then Cousin Rollo would pipe up: *As long as they don't tear down St. Pat's, I don't care about anything else.* And a female voice, maybe Mom or Aunt Elaine, *Give me the Chrysler Building any day. Now that's a work of art, all silvery and Art Deco...I always thought the twin towers were ridiculous, like two phallic monsters, but the young people loved them...You don't think the Chrysler is even more phallic? I mean look at the shape at the top....*

And as long as one was remembering, it was probably just as well to remember Grandma snubbing her estranged husband—she wouldn't think of getting an actual divorce, too shocking at the time for solid, middle-class folks, even if her father was a whoremaster deluxe with his Raines Law hotel, renting out rooms to hookers. Poor Grandpa Roth, on a dim snowy twilight on lower Fifth, he had called out to Grandma from the other side of the street, trying to get her attention. *Else! Else! Elsie!* And she kept on walking. *I couldn't speak to him, don't you see?* Trying to explain to Mom about something that had happened on a December day in 1922. And by January 1923, he was in his grave at Green-wood. He had either died of alcoholism or committed suicide. Which was it?

Christian let the music cover any attempt at small talk. Francine already knew Castillie had had a bad spell the night before, running out nude into the road and singing *It's a long way to Tipperary* at the top of her lungs in a fake Cockney accent. Her supposedly soft, meek little voice was completely *faux. Faux voice, faux person.* Apparently, no neighbors had witnessed her drugged-up madness. Christian said there was just an elderly lesbian couple next door. Occasionally he heard the piano and some loud singing, even some angry shouting. They appeared to be oblivious to other people's problems.

Francine and Christian knew each other far too well to bother being merely conversational. And the Beatles kept Francine grounded. She was glad of their gentle philosophy. They didn't go around killing people, did they? They let themselves get killed, one of them had. Big mistake. Happened right across the street from the Park

Royale. She even thought she had heard the shot from around the corner at the front entrance. *Eleanor Rigby...all the lonely people...*Ray Charles singing the song in his scratchy, heartbroken voice.

Lost in thought, blue sparkle winking madly just in front of her eyes, Francine didn't at first hear Christian's question: *I thought you were going to be a writer. Whatever happened to that plan? I remember you read aloud some pornographic story to your English Composition class at Hunter that shocked the pants off the other women...Oh I still write—sometimes, sometimes for Percie...May I remind you, Francine, that Percie's dead?*

The cousins then rode in silence until they reached the Montauk end of Long Island.

I wonder where she's gotten to, Christian said as the car tires crunched across the gravel driveway. No sign of Castillie anywhere.

Francine suggested she might have gone and drowned herself in the ocean just beyond. Christian said she was too lazy to exert that much effort. To drown yourself, you had to start walking into the waves which would then keep battering you, lifting you, washing you back onto the shore. Finally, after battling the tide for awhile, you might succeed in actually getting into them, under them, defeating their purpose of tossing you onto the shore like a rejected whale.

But not you, Christian said, looking Francine up and down, *you're too little. Too small and too quick.* Francine wondered, watching Christian's biceps bulge just a trifle as he lifted her brick-laden carryon out of the trunk, if he were hoping to fuck her. She wouldn't mind. She remembered Christian liked swift, intense fucks. Unlike Percie and his fleshly meanderings across her body—couldn't tell her nipple from her labia—that sometimes ended in a drunken bust with tears and apologies. It had been 20 years...years in which Percie dawdled along, as Solomon described it in the Bible, like an ox to the slaughter with a dart in his liver.

They finally found Castillie in the pantry, eating graham crackers out of the box, stuffing her big body, body grown heavier than ever, with grahams. Now she was unscrewing the grape jelly jar, prying open a small tub of margarine, messily smearing the crackers with jelly and mushy yellow stuff. Pressing this soft stuff against the cracker, Castillie made it split into several pieces, most of them falling to the floor, one of which she stuffed into her mouth. *Oh hi, Francine.* Speaking around the cracker, crumbs dribbling from between her teeth. *Haven't seen* **you** *in awhile...Hi Castillie....*

Francine slowly unpacked her carryon on the bed in the room assigned to her. It was on the far side of the cottage, at a discreet distance from the other two bedrooms. She suspected Christian and Castillie no longer slept in the same room.

She had to admit it was pleasant to be here in this cool room with the ocean a vague faraway lapping sound through the open window. She could see another house, much smaller, almost a hovel, in the distance and what appeared to be a small female figure working at an easel. Francine took the bricks out of her carryon and stashed them in the back of the closet.

Being in Christian's house was making her think more than ever about Percie and all the houses she'd been in with the two brothers. There'd been the old house on Soundview Drive in Greenwich, the Federal row house on W. 11th St. in the Village, her parents' Inwood apartment...even a big house in Fanwood New Jersey where Grandma Roth had lived with a man she'd met on the Hudson River Dayliner and then married...all the Roth homes, there seemed a myriad of them scattered about the "tri-state area" as the TV weather people called it.

Later that evening, around midnight, after Christian had doled out her Nembutol and Castillie had fallen asleep, he and Francine sat out in brightly-striped sling chairs under the trees on the scrappy, sandy back "lawn" and talked about Percie. In the dark, Christian's face looked almost saturnine. It was like having social intercourse with the devil. Francine sucked hard on her vodka martini, trying not to zone out completely as she listened to what Christian had to say about his brother. He was saying again that Percie had been a very frightened person all his life. It was the very same conversation they'd had many times over the years about Percie.

And Francine had her story: *I remember once when Percie was visiting us up in Inwood. He fell on the sidewalk and scraped his knee, blood started streaming down his leg, and he ran screaming with terror into our apartment house—* 'I'm dying! I'm dying!' *The elevator man brought him up to our apartment—we were in 4C then—and Mom had to put iodine on his knee and I had to hold him so she could do it. And then we tried to quiet him down. Mom finally gave him a big bowl of chocolate pudding smothered with whipped cream. That quieted him down immediately. Just give him some food and Percie was happy...*

Christian drained his martini and set the glass on the ground. *He never changed much in that regard. Only he went from food to booze.* Christian stretched and yawned, grabbing at a lowering tree branch and pulling off a handful of dusty leaves. *The only place Percie was sure of himself was on the baseball field. He actually had a baseball scholarship to Columbia, if you can imagine such a thing. I remember being really awed by him, watching him play ball up at Baker Field, the pride and joy of his team. His batting records there weren't broken for years, about 20, I think. He almost made it to the majors. Our Dad guided him every step of the way...Maybe that was the trouble...Oh yeah, you know how domineering Dad could be...I remember you got away from Uncle Henry as fast as you could, Christian. Percie once told me he really envied my durability. But I would never have let my parents bully me the way Uncle Henry bullied Percie. It wasn't their style anyway. Mom and Daddy were too involved with their own melodrama to bother that much with me. I actually never thought much about Percie's athleticism, except maybe in bed!* Christian laughed. Francine was remembering what a powerful body Percie had had as a young man.

Athleticism was the heart of him, Christian told her, *his dreaming heart that he almost fulfilled...I think, Christian, the trouble was Percie always wanted to have a good time...Yes, that came first. It was to get out from under Dad...You got out from under, why couldn't he?...We were different. There's no real explanation. We're born that way, I don't care what anyone says.* Christian hauled himself out of the chair with a yawn. *Hey, lady, want another martini?...No, thanks. You go to bed if you want. I'd like to just sit out here for awhile…Don't let the dampness get you. Oh, and if you hear Castillie stirring in the night, if she comes wandering into your room, which I doubt she will, the Nembutal takes care of that—well, just lead her by the hand back into her room.*

So it was true they slept in separate rooms. Francine smiled into the darkness.

Oh Christian, one thing, who's your neighbor? An artist? I have no idea. I haven't paid any attention. But go ahead and get acquainted, if you like. I don't want you to get too bored…With you around? I don't think so. Christian laughed and patted her on the shoulder. *Any time you want a massage, just yell.*

Chapter Five

Another evening in the backyard. Sun starting to go down, leaves rustling, distant slap and ripple of surf on shore. Christian and Francine side by side in the canvas sling chairs. A glass jug of Stoly martinis on the low table between them. Christian eyeing her intently. He was good at that kind of look.

Hey, look, Christian, there's that woman again at her easel. Let's go over and speak to her. Be neighborly, sort of...You go. I want to check on Castillie...Oh fuck that, come with me. Please. Christian thought about it...*Okay. I guess she's got enough Nembutal in her to last the night.*

They joined hands and crossed the field that separated the two properties. The woman looked up as they approached her. She smiled at them. *There's hardly any light left. Guess it's time to pack up and go in.* She had a low, soft voice with a pleasant intonation. Francine thought, *Miss Spence's school or a place like it.*

They introduced themselves. Gatty was a tiny woman, bowed deeply in the spine. She weighed perhaps 70 pounds. Her pale, lined face was still pretty. Her name was Gaither. Southern name. Gatty for short. Francine peeked at the painting on the easel, a colorful picture, mostly in primary colors, of several small dogs gathered at the bank of a rippling stream with their pink tongues hanging out. Francine thought these small creatures had a rather sassy, sarcastic air about them...much like Gatty. And pleasing to the eye.

Then from inside came a harsh shriek, like the cry of an animal in great pain. ***Gatty! Gatty! Gatsby!***

Gatsby? Francine sensed some playfulness between the two women.

Gatty shrugged and raised her voice slightly to reply. *I'm out here, Sybil! What do you want?* No answer from the raging animal inside the house. *I can hit her and beat her and scream at her,* Gatty told them, *and nothing does any good...Why don't you just kill her?* was Francine's question. *No one would know the difference 'way out here.* Gatty smiled. *Is that what you'd do?* She ran paint-stained fingers through her coarse mop of curly white hair. *Come to think of it, I might do that yet.*

Gatty was folding her easel and packing her paints and brushes and rags. *Please come in and meet Sybil. It'll be fun. Not meeting her, I mean, because she's become such an old horror, but we'll have fun talking. It'll be neighborly, right?...That's just what I said to Christian...* Gatty promised, *We'll have tea.*

Christian shrugged, then surprised Francine by agreeing. They followed Gatty into the house. *Would you like some tea?*

Tea! What a novel idea. *You mustn't go to any trouble.* As Christian and Francine followed Gatty through the back door and then a screened-in porch, she shouted nervously. *Sybil! Where are you? We've got guests! Put your clothes on! It's teatime!*

An old lady, even more bent than Gatty, emerged from the shadows. Wearing a blue sweatshirt emblazoned on the chest with LIBERIA in big red block letters, black sweatpants and yellow high-topped sneakers, grinned at them out of an alarmingly toothless mouth. *Would you like a song while Gatty brews the tea?* Her voice was amazingly soft and civilized for an "old horror". Then she sat down at the old upright, strummed a few evocative chords—at least the piano was in tune—and began singing in a loud broken voice. *Falling in love again, never wanted to. What am I to do? I can't help it....?* It was the old Marlene Dietrich song. Francine wondered if Sybil had ever looked like Dietrich. Sybil's eighty-year-old blue eyes matched the cornflowers in the back yard. As Francine stared at her, Sybil's tee-shirt sagging far down her curved spine, Gatty spoke softly. *I always loved her beautiful back.* Francine imagined them young and in love with each other, Gatty stroking Sybil's beautiful fleshy back, now grown loose and spare, no man in the picture for awhile. Gatty spoke again. *I used to ride my bike clear across town from E. 86th Street to Chelsea every night to be with her.*

Francine and Christian sat side by side on a blue velvet sofa, hemmed in by a long coffee table made up of a marble slab mounted on four concrete blocks. From there they could look across the room through large windows to the back garden, Gatty's workplace, alive in the twilight with rosebushes and the masses of blue cornflowers. A monstrous density of purple-blue moonflowers climbed up trellises at odd intervals along the yard, like a Dali dream painting. Beyond lay the ocean. Christian clutched Francine's hand and squeezed it. He was excited. The strange enchantment.

Sybil stopped and swiveled around on the piano stool. *I lost my voice. I had an accident to my larynx with a broken glass. They had to operate. My voice was never the same. It has a certain hoarseness to it.*

Gatty told them later that some crazed and raging lover had broken a beer bottle and rammed the jagged edge into Sybil's throat during a bar brawl.

Sybil swiveled back to the keyboard and the song. *Love's always been my game... play it how I may... I was made that way... I can't hel-l-l-l-p it...*

Gatty returned with the tea tray and set it on the coffee table. Sybil paused long enough in her song to holler, *Shouldn't you be serving coffee on a coffee table?...Shut up, Sybil!* The old lady cackled and continued her song. *Men cluster 'round me like moths around a flame... and if their wings burn... I know I'm not to blame....*

There were cups, saucers, teaspoons, paper napkins, a pot of tea, sugar cookies...*I made them myself to help Sybil's indigestion. I can't stand it. Sometimes I can't stand to hear her shitting and moaning in the bathroom...* Sybil lurched to the table sailor-style to get a cookie. *Are you a doctor?* she asked Christian. He shook his head. *You look like a doctor. Can you die from taking too much Metamucil? No that's not the name of it.* **Gatty!** *What's the name of that over the counter junk I take for diarrhea? The name starts with an M. I think....* Christian tried to be helpful. *Too much of any medicine will kill you sooner or later.* Sybil accepted this wisdom graciously and went into the kitchen, coming back with a can of generic supermarket beer. Gatty wrinkled her nose, staring at the beer can. *All right. Whatever...Beer isn't really booze, Gatty. It's more like a food. When my grandmother had typhoid malaria and lost 40 pounds, the doctor made her drink beer every day...When was this, in the Middle Ages? In Lower Slobovia? Where, Sybil?*

Did they put leeches on her, too?...Leeches are good, Gatty. I just read about them in Newsday. *They're used for infections. They put them on a badly-infected lip and they suck out the poison and heal the wound at the same time... Please, Sybil, we're trying to eat.*

Sybil went back to the piano. *A Dietrich specialist,* Francine thought, as Sybil launched into a sad German song written for those who have loved and lost. *Leben ohne lieben, kannst du nicht?* Francine wondered if she could live without Percie's love, his half-love, the sweet baby love that she'd spent a lifetime trying to extract from him. Sybil followed with the snappier *Mein blondes baby....* Francine remembered from reading a book about Dietrich that she had been dumped by the French actor "tough guy" Jean Gabin after their long, hot affair, and it had broken her heart. He'd been the love of her life. But how many hearts had *she* broken?

Francine could understand Marlene's attraction to Gabin, the same one she herself felt for the prototypical squint-eyed, pock-marked gangster, the guy with a pack of Camels rolled up in his biceps-revealing short-sleeved tee-shirt, the latter-day Harvey Keitels, the Tommy Lee Joneses, a gun symbolically tucked into the back of their waistbands. Oddly, Percie didn't fit the prototype, not that soft, sluggish ball of blond fur. But Christian did, if not in appearance, then in essence. Something saturnine in his thin face, something sinister....Or was it all in her mind? Perpetually making of each twin something that wasn't there.

Later, lying with Christian on his big bed, Francine asked *What was your take on those two?...Sybil seems somewhat demented, probably just her age...Maybe. I really like Gatty, though. She'd be okay without Sybil ...Maybe...On the other hand—* Francine snuggled closer to Christian—*I love Sybil's songs...Yeah, she's quite an old gal...Think she's had many lovers?...We'll find out, won't we, Francine?*

From Christian's bed, they could look through the bathroom doors that led to Castillie's bedroom, could even see her bloated form under the bedsheet. She was snoring. Or strangling. It was a prolonged, ugly sound. They kept listening to her snores, to make sure she was still snoring, before they turned to each other and began silently, softly kissing each other on the lips, at the same time holding onto each other's hands as they had in childhood. Then, without warning, Christian smacked her ass hard and Francine let out a little scream. She'd forgotten how deliciously cruel he could be in bed, with a sharp smack that effectively opened her up to his gifted fucking.

Castillie stopped snoring and they jerked away from each other for a moment, fearful their noise had awakened her. Then with a moaning, gulping sound she began coughing. Silence. Then she was snoring again. Christian murmured incoherently against Francine's neck.

The hair on his sleek body was still black and crisp, the same as when he was young, standing bare-chested on the diving board at the Indian Harbor Yacht Club, showing off his diving prowess by taking powerful, purposeful flight into the pool below. *Always playing second fiddle to Percie in the area of sports,* Francine thought. She fondled his handsome, yearning cock with one hand, his sleek olive cheek with the other. Then she realized Christian was crying. She fingered the tears on his cheek. *It doesn't seem right without Percie here beside us.* He was swallowing sobs. *I've lost my brother,* he moaned. *He was ambidextrous, you know. He could bat left-handed or right-handed. He could pitch with both hands. People who are ambidextrous are crazy, did you know that?*

Suddenly from the inner region of the next door cottage came the raucous shouting of the Marlene-Dietrich-in-residence with *The a-larm-ing, the charm-ing blonde women!* The piano was banging a martial accompaniment. *You try in vain, you can't explain, the charming blonde women!...You're facing danger....*

Francine giggled aloud, then squeezed her hand against her mouth for fear she had awakened the comatose Castillie. Christian laughingly picked up the rhythm and began fucking Francine to completion in the properly rhythmical strokes. *The a-**larm**-ing, the **charm**-ing blonde **wo**-men!...And I'm not even a blonde woman,* Francine murmured as she felt an orgasm spreading through her body like surf spreading, silent and irredeemable, across the shore. *I prefer brunettes, petite brunettes,* Christian muttered gallantly, rushing into her.

Christian continued with his own train of thought. *So is that why you rejected me in favor of Percie?* He didn't wait for an answer. *You know, Percie and I were fraternal twins, not identical twins. I was the skinny one. Percie weighed thirteen pounds when he was born, too big for our little mother, you think. On the contrary, Percie's soft head came easily down the birth canal—and out—while my hard head tore her up down there. They had to do an episiotomy. Or maybe that just paved the way for Percie's smooth sailing out of her body...Yes, you looked completely different. I always thought of you as the evil Cassius in* Julius Caesar. *Or maybe Iago...*

Christian laughed. *I'm really a pussycat...I don't think so...You've got it all wrong, Francine. Percie was the bad one. And all those fake suicide attempts. The one he tried to pull off on the highway driving up to Boston, the pills he claimed he'd hoarded so that he could turn off into some hypothetical woods someplace and swallow them all. And then just ignominiously, getting arrested for drunk driving and losing his license.*

Behaving badly toward women, getting thrown out of bars. Sometimes he would get up on top of the bars and dance with the crazy young bare-assed women showing off, pulling down his pants, making a drunken spectacle of himself.

For Francine the memory was different. She remembered Percie dancing for her amusement in Aunt Elaine's and Uncle Henry's long living room in Greenwich, his big heavy hams of feet placed as prettily and precisely as any ballerina's as he whirled in a series of pirouettes or angled his arms in one direction and his legs in another in a gracefully sloping arabesque.

Christian had more to say about Percie, whether out of jealousy or heartbreak for his twin's broken life, Francine could not say. *Percie was a failed athlete, couldn't make it to the Majors. It wasn't just that drunken car crash that broke his back. The Cubs organization saw early on he was a drunk, admired by his false friends, other drunks, for his prodigious drinking. Later, riding back to Long Island on the train with a group who called themselves Alcoholics Unanimous. All very funny. And sad, really. Ha ha. You don't know all the things my poor brother did, the hearts he broke without knowing it, and sometimes knowing it, apparently including yours.*

Christian continued. *And remember how he used to screw up his eyes and his mouth when he laughed, those supposedly merry glints in his eyes like the Merry Prankster, like Tyl Eulenspiegel, his laughing eyes really mocking and hostile. And then, of course, he made himself insane with drink. I hated living with his hangovers, his vomit, his excuses, his DTs, his delusive bouts in the hospital with alcoholic poisoning...You make Percie sound repulsive...I hope so...*Francine protested. *He was once adorable and cute.* Christian began kissing her again, murmuring into her face between kisses. She lifted her hand to his hair, still springy and black. *You picked the wrong twin to go into a lifelong frenzy over. I'm the one you should love,* he said. And just as Francine was thinking she would try to love Christian as hard as she could because he was her last link with Percie, that's when they heard Castillie's screech at their open door. She had seen them in each other's arms while they had become oblivious to her snores alternating with her silence in the other bedroom.

Christian tore out of bed but Castillie was too quick for him. She was running out the back door, huge, but agile in her sheer pink beribboned nightgown, headed for the beach, shrieking incoherently as she went. *Let her go,* Francine called after him in a tired voice. She had seen a hint of dawn creeping along the back lawn and realized they'd been lying in Christian's bed all night. Insufficient Nembutal in Castillie's system. *She'll be back...*Clearly Christian, usually so decisive, so resolute, could not decide whether to pursue his wife. *This isn't good, Francine. God knows what she'll do.* He was tugging on jeans and a sweatshirt. *This is the first time she's ever caught me. I've always been so careful...What's the matter, do you still love her?...*Christian was panting. *I suppose so. We've been together so long...*They were now shouting at each other, raging at each other in guilty terror. *Does that make for love?...I don't know. I remember her—as a young woman. She was beautiful and—sweet.* Now he was pulling on socks and boots. *I'm afraid she'll try to drown herself. She's tried before...Oh, is that why you live at the edge of the Atlantic?* Christian winced. And Francine was remembering the silly-looking teenager with the masses of kinky blonde hair she'd seen him with at Percie's funeral. Had he brought *her* out to Montauk for fuck sessions?

Christian could no longer speak. She had never seen him so frantic, his face grey and wild. And old. Every inch his 69 years! When all was said and done, he still cared about his wife. Maybe that's what love was.

Francine remembered Christian's description of someone trying to drown...He had said it took an immense effort to drown yourself, that the waves kept battering you back and that eventually you would be beached like a huge whale. Castillie would certainly make a wonderful big pink whale lying stranded on the shore, waves lapping at her generously, rolling across her ass.

The blue light flickered, and flickered again, this time more vividly—*color of a dress I want*, she thought wantonly, *color of a ring*—and Francine felt dizzy for a moment.

She dressed herself and followed slowly in Christian's wake. Dawn was still leaking out of the East; it wouldn't stop. She thought she saw a pink whale bobbing up and down helplessly on the rolling, crashing waves perhaps a hundred yards from shore. Surely Christian would not attempt to swim out there in a futile attempt to save Castillie! If she were really drowned, wouldn't she be down in the ocean deeps? Or perhaps she was like a gigantic inner tube that couldn't help floating, and then would float into shore.

Christian was running helplessly up and down the beach, facing the grisly dawn—an overlay of dark clouds with pale sunlight trying to breach the darkness. Gatty was running toward them from up the beach. Her clothes were wet, sopping, dripping with seawater. *I tried to get to her,* she yelled as though her voice were jammed, her heart filling up her throat. *I thought at first she just wanted to cool off in the water, but she kept going. Then I realized....* Gatty stared at them pleadingly as though she felt she were personally responsible for Castillie's behavior. *I'm so sorry...*She pointed wordlessly, futilely, her finger wavering, at the pink whale borne up one moment and then down the other on the roiling water. *There she is! I think at the last minute she* *changed her mind. She was trying to get out of the water. I'm sure she was.*

From next door came Sybil's hoarse, throat-damaged yell. *Gatty! I called 9-1-1! They're coming!*

Now there were other people around, a man in a small boat rowing ferociously toward the distant pink blob. Strangers swarmed the beach like ants drawn to a cluster of crumbs. Police cars pulled to the side of the road. Men in blue ran out. *What's going on? We got a call, a woman drowning?* After them came an ambulance, a fire truck, another medical truck, the official emergency trucks of disaster and death. They would remain there throughout most of the day until it was clear there could be no rescuing of Castillie.

Gatty had been out there on the shore collecting seashells for a collage.

Francine was losing sight of the pink blob. The waves proved too rough for the small boat. Its owner said later he had lost sight of her. A few minutes later a Coast Guard boat, white and sleek, motored across the horizon and circled the area for a long time, all day. Francine counted the minutes and then the hours by the chugging of the boat, the dip and sway of its gleaming boards in and out of the frothing waves. Christian sat huddled at water's edge, his face in his hands. He had taken off his shoes and socks when he thought he might be able to wade out and help Castillie. Now as he sat huddled, surf curled over his bare toes. A cop squatted beside him, taking notes. The tide was low now and a light mist danced above the water. Gulls squawked and flapped overhead, keening across the pink sky.

All day, as Christian and Francine kept watch on the beach, Gatty and Sybil brought them drinks and food. Other neighbors tiptoed across the sand with blankets and pillows. Christian cried intermittently, saying he had failed his wife. There was little anyone could do in the wake of the horror. Francine felt her heartbeats dwindling. How many were left to her? As she hugged and kissed her cousin, she felt her heart hurting so bad, growing too big for her chest, thumping with Christian's misery. She promised her heart that from now on, she would love Christian as hard as she could.

Eventually Gatty's collage became a grotesque tribute to Castillie's death by drowning, a collage made up of sand, shells, bits of driftwood, leaves of rusty seaweed, all dyed a deep purple, with big, round moonflower petals and a tiny replica of a white skull with a hank of red hair protruding from one earhole, the hank of hair Gatty had salvaged from Castillie's actual body after it washed up, days later, a mile or so down the shoreline.

Late afternoons now Francine and Christian went frequently next door to Gatty's house for tea or beer or whatever was on the menu. Sometimes Francine made an Alsatian specialty.

We're Alsatian-Americans, Francine told the women, *just like German-Americans, Italian-Americans, or African-Americans. Only you never hear about us...That's because there are so few of us left,* Christian said. *There used to be more of us but with intermarriage and dispersal—our particular Roth line is pretty much played out.*

Crumbling sugar cookies into her stein of beer, Sybil said there had been a Nazi concentration camp in Alsace in the '40s where parents of a friend had been killed. *Struthof, I think that was the name of it. Are the Alsatians as cruel as the Germans?...*Gatty said every nation had its cruel people. She sipped her tea slowly. *There are many ways of killing people.*

Sybil asked, *Isn't Roth a Jewish name?...*Christian explained. *Our family was Catholic.*

Francine often brought to Gatty's house an Ammerschwihr specialty from Grandma Roth's recipe book. One such was *noix au roquefort*—made from roquefort, sweet butter, brandy, walnut meats and capers. Or a steaming dinner platter of the better known *choucroute garni*—cabbage and sausage—along with a six-pack of Sybil's favorite generic beer and a bottle of Alsatian *pinot gris* from Christian's cellar.

Sybil played her Marlene Dietrich songs over and over, the rousing *Ich bin die fesche Lola!* Or the teasingly poignant *Allein in einer grossen Stadt* that took Francine back to her days of prowling Europe, lost in immense, dimly-lit glass-topped train stations like gigantic movie studios being prepared for a shoot, climbing onto a train in Milan headed for Zurich at the very last minute, waiting for her man, Ray or Percie or some other male companion, to board the train, hoping he wouldn't miss it while lost reading a magazine.

Back at Christian's house where Castillie's ghost had begun to wander in red-haired apathy—Francine caught glimpses of her passing quickly through a closed door or shimmying along the bedroom wall as her husband and Francine made love—the message machine came on with a whirr and a start and spoke to the empty, hag-haunted house. *Hello, Mom, it's your son Larry. Remember me? I finally unearthed Christian's phone number after I found out your phone in New York was disconnected. And I wondered if you yourself had finally become disconnected. Ha ha. That's supposed to be a joke! Please call me. I'm planning a trip East. I miss you, though God knows why. I don't think you've* ever *missed me. But I love you, Mom.*

The blue light continued to flicker. Some day soon, when death overtook her, the blue light would stop flickering. Meanwhile she and Christian would stay together, their two half-dead lives making a whole.

Lying quietly in the dark next to Christian, thinking about Percie and wishing he were there, she was startled by a high noise in her stomach, like the sudden outcry of a baby in its sleep. She had never heard anything like it, never. She smiled, remembering her little son Larry from long ago. At the end.

CHOO-CHOO, A CASE STUDY

I've talked to many women who've been molested in childhood by family members or others in authority. They feel their adult sex lives have been irreparably harmed by these events. Then there are others who openly admit the pleasure they derived from these taboo encounters. I am among the latter group of "abused" children, presently living with a great guy, Leo, who physically resembles in the stockiness of his well-muscled body and in the sensual features of his broad face the step-grandfather who seduced me when I was 13.

The real world gradually ebbs away as Leo's hands work their relentless discipline on me, digging deep between my legs where you can hear the sloshing of my juices, the sound we both enjoy as an affirmation of our passion, paralyzing my senses and transporting me to another time, another place. I am lying in the second floor bedroom of my grandfather, my step-grandfather Carlos, that is, since my real grandfather chose to kill himself four years before I was born. I am in a golden place. Sun streams in through the windows of his palatial estate outside Santiago, Cuba. Giant palms on the back lawn cast fan-shaped shadows on the window shades, fluttering slightly in chiaroscuro, making the reddish black tones of the mahogany bureau, night table and huge four-poster bed shimmer silkily, memorializing my initiation at age 13 into the miraculous tyranny of shared sex.

I've been thinking about Choo-Choo a lot lately. I spent many happy childhood hours in his playroom where he had an enormous and elaborate setup of miniature trains. So passionate was he about these 0-scale imitation steam trains, his friends called him Choo-Choo.

He was a corrupt government official high in Castro's regime and therefore living like a king. If he wanted to enjoy the body of his little granddaughter nightly, who was to stop him? Of course, I was the little princess who lusted after him mightily and therefore didn't bother to tell anyone about our carnal relationship.

I'll admit I didn't enjoy Choo-Choo right away. It took some forceful "courtship" on his part for me to learn to enjoy his body. The fact that he was my step-grandfather also blocked my sexual responses for awhile. I realized we weren't related by blood, but even so he was the only grandfather I'd ever known because

Mama's father was dead. Choo-Choo had been in our family since before I was born. He had rocked me in the cradle, given me baths, and even once an enema when I had a high fever and there was no one else around to care for me.

Now as I fondle Leo's cock in the aftermath of our lovemaking, I think back many years to a morning in June....

Choo-Choo makes me wait a long time as he performs his ablutions in the adjacent bathroom. I imagine his stocky, muscular body growing pink under the steaming shower. This is the glowing body that will soon consume mine. His rough grey-white stubble of beard will scratch hot images of power and plenitude on my tender asscheeks as the sharp point of his reptilian pink tongue seeks my tight anal opening .

Now I'm in Leo's arms again, this man who heads a large corporation and whom I've recently come to live with. Leo could be a clone of Choo-Choo, as his tongue—a butterfly's gentle wing—moves along the line from my anus to my genitals. Choo-Choo's tongue, Leo's tongue, whose it it? I climax in response, not to a single lover, but to an entire concept of eroticism as embodied in the power of either, or both, of these men. A woman in her 40s and I'm as wet as a teenager. What can I say? I'm susceptible to sex. I always have been...from earliest childhood.

It started at Juanita's house when I was four years old. She was just a year older than I. One hot summer afternoon Mama had our chauffeur drive us across town to where Juanita and her family lived. Mama was a good friend of Juanita's mother. When we arrived, the two mothers sat in the parlor with cups of tea and I was sent to play with Juanita and her older friend in the playroom. For a few seconds I stood just inside the half open door. The two little girls were whispering together and looking at me from the other side of the room. Then they came over to me and told me to lie down on the child-size kitchen table. I did as I was told. Juanita pulled my legs apart and took hold of my forefinger and put it between my legs, rubbing it back and forth within the tender folds of my labia. Then she held my finger to my nose for me to smell. It made me very excited. I didn't want it to stop. I was in the grip of some strange force that made me throb between my legs. But I was fearful Mama would come in and see what we were doing. That was all part of the excitement. Sex was taboo. I was having sex. I was doing something wrong that I loved doing. I kept craning my neck to watch the door in case Mama should come in suddenly. The air in the bright playroom grew very still. The other girls continued abusing me with my own fingers. My aroma drove me wild. The stimulation they were giving me was almost unbearable.

The following year, at the age of five, I fell in love with a twelve-year-old boy who lived next door to us and whose mother was also a close friend of Mama's. Once when we were visiting, Manuel rolled me up in a rug the maid had put out on the back patio for airing and only God knows what he intended to do after that because Mama came running out of the house to rescue me. It was always this way with me. I was in love time after time as I grew older, usually with some classmate with whom I could play stink-finger in a vacant lot or under the boardwalk at the beach.

Then came the summer when I was 13, visiting my grandparents which Mama evidently considered a perfectly safe place for me to be. My grandfather's inexorable pursuit of his own bliss held me captive. He enslaved me before I knew what was happening. It began innocently for me. Yet he had apparently noted something in my demeanor that gave him the notion I wouldn't resist him completely. I had visited them the previous year accompanied by Mamacita—my maternal grandmother who lived with us. This particular year, Abuela Luisa said she wanted me all to herself. I suspect Choo-Choo put the idea in her head. He rightly figured he could have his way with me without Mamacita around to stand guard.

I was a well-protected little girl until the summer I found myself at the house in Santiago. It went something like this:

Dios mio, here comes Choo-Choo. I wonder if he's going to try to kiss me again. He waits until I come downstairs to the secluded courtyard shaded by huge potted trees…while Abuela Luisa is still upstairs getting ready for our evening outing. With one eye rolled toward the stairway and an ear cocked for her footsteps, Choo-Choo darts toward me and presses a wet, bristly kiss on my mouth. I stand still. He steps back with a sigh. Then he reaches out again to touch my head. "Would you say your hair is a chestnut color?"

"I don't know." I stand very still, waiting for him to stop.

After dinner—we always go out to dinner when I stay with them—the three of us stand on the sidewalk in front of the restaurant. Choo-Choo wants to buy my first bra for me. "What size do you wear?"

"I don't know."

"Is it like this?" He cups imaginary oranges at his chest.

Abuela Luisa laughs and hits at his hands. "Not here, Carlos," she protests. How can she be so blind about what's going on? They walk toward the car. I follow, looking around me. The street is almost deserted. The sun is going down. The trees rustle in the warm air. Otherwise, it's very still. I wonder when he'll make his next move on me....

It happens quite suddenly. One day I'm a sweet little virgin, the next day I'm not. And after Choo-Choo had picked my cherry and eaten it, I had to continue for years pretending to my parents that I was innocent. I had to pretend to be excited about going to my first boy-girl party and having my books carried home every afternoon by the gawky, snickering boys in my class. We would sit on the verandah and Mama would send the maid out to us with cold drinks and snacks.

This pretense that I was a virgin was all fantasy. I'd been fucking Grandpa since I was 13. He'd nailed me soon after my first menstrual period. Somehow my parents had never caught on to this. I guess they couldn't conceive of a 13-year-old girl enjoying being fucked by a 59-year-old man. My parents played the traditional role of welcoming my friends to our house, talking to my so-called boyfriends and putting their stamp of approval on one or the other—or not. Mama would let me know in no uncertain terms whether I could continue seeing one or another of my escorts. I was never without a date to take me to the movies or out for a syrupy ice at a local café. Then there was the usual rather innocent kiss goodnight at my front door.

At first I didn't enjoy kissing Choo-Choo so I usually avoided mouth to mouth contact with him. I was used to the smooth-cheeked boys at school or in my social dancing class. These boys were sons of the privileged high officials of Castro's regime. They seemed very bland compared to Choo-Choo. The perpetual stubble of his beard was harsh on my soft young face. I endured it on my thighs and belly when he went down on me because his tongue was like a magic wand, licking me to fulfillment.

I confess it, I live for sensation. I always have, even from early childhood. What a burden it was for Mama. I remember masturbating for several minutes in the bathtub with Mama standing outside the door nagging at me to get out before the water went cold. I was eight or nine years of age. It was January and the weather had gone unusually frigid for Cuba. I told her I was coming out, just a minute, I hadn't finished washing, I'd be out in a minute, etc. I continued to play with myself, pursuing the elusive orgasm. Mama kept nagging. "What are you doing in there? You'll catch cold. You've just gotten over one, now you're going get pneumonia!" I finally gave up. I wasn't going to achieve an orgasm. But it felt so good, working the firm, responsive young flesh of my labia and clitoris with my fingers while the lukewarm water bathed the action. I've always loved the water, another important sensual mode for me. If Narcissus couldn't resist his image in the pond, neither could I. Mama must have worried about the trances she often found me in. I was totally sex-oriented from the age of four.

Which is why Grandpa must have found me so attractive. He must have caught glimpses of a cuddly, dreamy little girl, one finger idling in her mouth, another sneaking into her panties for a surreptitious fondling of her clitoris. One evening Choo-Choo waited until Abuela Luisa went to bed. She always insisted I retire at 8:30. Then she went to bed in her room down the corridor. Pretty soon I heard a scratching at the door. It was Grandpa. I shivered in my nightgown as I went to open the door. He was wearing his long, satin brocade robe. As we stood staring at each other, the robe fell open to reveal his stocky, well-muscled body. A glance down at his crotch revealed his long, powerful cock that was slowly rising until it was perpendicular to the floor staring at me, its single eye seeming to wink. Oh my....

He put his finger to his lips, a silent admonition not to disturb Abuela. Then he pushed into the room and guided me back into the bed. He stretched himself out beside me. I was nervous, wondering what would happen next. Nothing happened. Pretty soon I heard his even breathing, saw that his eyes were closed tight, and realized he had fallen asleep. I did the same. The firm weight of his body was somehow comforting. I thought how nice it would be if he came in and slept with me every night, me under the covers, he on top of them.

Next day when we were once more waiting for Abuela to join us in the courtyard, Choo-Choo kissed me again. His beard didn't seem so scratchy this time. In fact, I rather enjoyed its harshness. It set my senses quivering and I could feel wetness in my vagina. I was thinking it would be nice if he joined me in bed again. The image of his cock appeared in my mind's eye and I had a sudden urge to offer one of my plump young breasts to his thin, rather cruel-looking mouth. I imagined how it would feel to have him mash the pink strawberry of my nipple between his lips. Then I saw Abuela Luisa approaching from the stairway. How silently she'd come up on us.

"Choo-Choo really loves you," she said in her whispery voice. She'd mistaken his kiss for one of affection.

"I know," I simpered, trying to act like a normal 13-year-old.

I was getting hot for Choo-Choo. That night I heard the same rustling at my bedroom as on the previous evening. This time I didn't go to the door. I waited for him to come in on his own. I stayed very still, hardly breathing. In a moment, I heard the slight wheeze of door hinges as Choo-Choo pushed his way in. As he approached the bed, his brocade dressing gown falling back to reveal his monstrous manhood, I couldn't help but pull the sheet 'way up over my face in a rush of maidenly modesty. Then I shuddered as he slowly pulled the sheet away and sat beside me, surveying my body, the virginal rounds of my breasts as they rose and fell under the thin cotton of my summer gown, the black hair of my Venus mound faintly visible through my nightie. I kept my eyes closed as he leaned over and kissed me softly. The night air hung heavy over us and we seemed to be suspended in a delicious limbo of expectation.

I felt his lips grazing my nipples where they pushed hungrily against the bodice of my nightgown. My cunt automatically lubricated itself. I was familiar with the feeling because I had been masturbating since the age of four, ever since my encounter with Juanita and her friend. I knew well the folds and crevices of my steaming sexual jungle and I knew the familiar sweet wetness that poured out when I aroused myself. Now I longed for Choo-Choo's fingers to ease my hunger and I waited for him to sneak them in under my gown. Instead, he lay down beside me and in a few minutes I could hear the gentle rhythmic breathing that indicated he was asleep. Tears of frustration seeped down under my eyelids and across my cheeks as I turned over and dipped my fingers into my still-steaming pussy hole. For some reason, I couldn't bring myself off. I needed Choo-Choo Carlos to do that.

I finally fell asleep. In the morning, Choo-Choo was gone and Abuela Luisa knocked at my door. "Sweetheart, your breakfast is ready," she called through the door in her wispy voice. It was ten o'clock. In spite of my frustration with Choo-Choo, I had slept well, remembering only once the weight of his body against mine when I awoke briefly in the night. Had I dreamed it or had I really felt his hand pressing my belly as we lay shaped together back to front like perfectly fitting spoons?

After breakfast, Choo-Choo called me down to the playroom where he worked on his trains. It was a massive layout, the tracks laid on wooden trestles that reached four feet off the plush carpeting that covered the floor. Choo-Choo suddenly turned rough. "Do you know what happens to naughty little girls who play with themselves when they think nobody is looking?" Before I could utter a word, he grabbed me by the shoulders and pushed me down beneath the trestles and dragged me into a far corner. This is where he'd piled cushions and pillows for his occasional naps or when he spent evenings alone drinking and watching the tiny TV under his layout. Down I went under his masterful hand. He reached under my skirt, yanked down my panties and ordered me to spread my legs, adding in his rough voice, "I felt the bed shaking last night. I knew what you were doing to yourself. You had your fingers between your legs, didn't you?" He clapped his free hand over my mouth so that when he precipitately plunged his enormous cock into my honey pit, he was able to stifle the cry of pain that burst from me. As he rode me in a hot, abrasive rhythm of lust, sliding up and down between my resisting walls, he continued his morality sermon.

"Good little girls don't play with their privates and certainly no granddaughter of mine is going to perform an immoral act!" He kept on taunting and scolding me as his engorged penis gathered energy and tension, preparing to discharge its load of semen into my seething hole. I glanced timidly up into his face. It was also engorged and red, in stern concentration on the rape of me that was making him so excited. With a great roar of satisfaction, he shot his load into me, then turned me over and proceeded to slap my asscheeks savagely. "Choo-Choo doesn't like his little girl doing naughty things. You must learn to control yourself." I was too stunned to reply. I know how pleasant it feels to be fucked," he continued, "but you must learn self discipline." After a moment, he rolled me over and tearing off my blouse so that my round fat breasts rolled out lazily, he began sucking my nipples, pressing both together and eagerly biting and licking them. He added, "Choo-Choo will help you to restrain yourself."

I wondered if he'd taken leave of his senses as he continued to suckle me, his fingers buried deep in my private parts, all the while sermonizing about how he wanted his granddaughter to comport herself. His soft, slow, teasing manipulation with its frequent stops and starts soon brought me to my own climax. Whether it was his masterful fingers slipping and sliding in my honey or the touch of his tongue on my clit, he opened me up until I was begging him to penetrate me again. When he again shoved his cock into me and began his rough, deep lunging in and out, I felt wave upon wave of orgasm sweep through my body.

Thus began my feverish relationship with Choo-Choo, he keeping up the myth that I was a bad little girl who initiated our physical intimacy. He claimed I never left him alone and constantly required him to service me, so that I needed frequent tongue-lashings and butt-whippings to keep me in my place. These beatings got fiercer as the days went by, as did his fucking of my ass, vaginal as well as anal. Choo-Choo was stretching my openings wider and wider. If I'd been more experienced and not essentially still a little girl, I would have wondered where all this was leading.

I began to worry about getting pregnant. Finally I approached Abuela Luisa, not with a declaration of fornication with her husband but with a question. "How come you and Choo-Choo never had children? Were you too old, Abuela?"

"No, querida. Choo-Choo went to Sweden for a vasectomy just before we were married. I felt I was too old to have more children. I've been content with your father as my only child."

I felt very relieved after this conversation. I'd had nightmares about mysteriously producing a child and not being able to explain its origin. The shame of my relationship with Choo-Choo went so deep I had a horror of admitting it to anyone. I didn't even tell my closest girlfriends, some of whom didn't yet know the facts of life. Until I became involved with my present lover Leo, my affair with Choo-Choo was the hottest affair of my life.

BIOGRAPHY

Patricia Hickerson grew up in NYC/Jersey, a Barnard graduate with a Masters in Creative Writing from San Francisco State; a doctorate from USC. Came to California in 1956. She has been a Warner Bros. dancer, artists' model, mother of three, teacher, reporter who started with poetry at age 7, much later reading her poetry in San Francisco bars and bookstores, selling pornography to various *Penthouse* publications such as *Forum, Letters, Erotica, Variations*. Her poems have been published in the chapbook *Dawn and Dirty* and the broadside *At Grail Castle Hotel*, both from Rattlesnake Press; other poems have been published in *Ten Pages Press* (an e-chap *Rachel, My Torment*), *Convergence, Medusa's Kitchen, poetrynow, Presa, Choices, Echoes, Passager, catfishgringoriver, Fitzroy Dreaming, poets for peace, poets for living waters, Rattlesnake Review, WTF, The Yolo Crow* and *The Ophidian*.

www.ingramcontent.com/pod-product-compliance
Lightning Source LLC
Chambersburg PA
CBHW020514100426
42813CB00030B/3244/J